Philip Ri

Radiant Vermin

Bloomsbury Methuen Drama
An imprint of Bloomsbury Publishing Plc

B L O O M S B U R Y
LONDON • NEW DELHI • NEW YORK • SYDNEY

Bloomsbury Methuen Drama
An imprint of Bloomsbury Publishing Plc

Imprint previously known as Methuen Drama

50 Bedford Square	1385 Broadway
London	New York
WC1B 3DP	NY 10018
UK	USA

www.bloomsbury.com

Bloomsbury is a registered trade mark of Bloomsbury Publishing Plc

First published 2015

© Philip Ridley 2015

British Library Cataloguing-in-Publication Data
A catalogue record for this book is available from the British Library.

ISBN: PB: 978-1-4742-5150-1
ePub: 978-1-4742-5153-2
ePDF: 978-1-4742-5152-5

Library of Congress Cataloging-in-Publication Data
A catalog record for this book is available from the Library of Congress.

Typeset by Mark Heslington Ltd, Scarborough, North Yorkshire
Printed and bound in Great Britain

Metal Rabbit & Supporting Wall
present

Radiant Vermin
by Philip Ridley

World Premiere

Tobacco Factory Theatres, Bristol
27 February – 7 March 2015

Soho Theatre, London
10 March – 12 April 2014

METAL
RABBIT

supporting
wall

Radiant Vermin
by Philip Ridley

Cast

Jill	Gemma Whelan
Ollie	Sean Michael Verey
Miss Dee	Amanda Daniels

Director	David Mercatali
Design & lighting	William Reynolds
Assistant director	Hannah Hauer-King
Production manager	Heather Doole
Company stage manager	Hannah Royall

Produced by	George Warren & Martha Rose Wilson for Metal Rabbit Productions
	Ben Monks & Will Young for Supporting Wall

Supported by Arts Council England, Unity Theatre Trust, Andrew Smith MP and Lord Baker.

Presented by kind permission of the Knight Hall Agency Limited of Lower Ground Floor, 7 Mallow Street, London EC1Y 8RQ.

Philip Ridley

Philip was born in the East End of London where he still lives and works. He studied painting at St Martin's School of Art and his work has been exhibited widely throughout Europe and Japan. As well as three books for adults – and the highly acclaimed screenplay for *The Krays* (winner of the *Evening Standard* Best Film of the Year Award) – he has written ten adult stage plays: *The Pitchfork Disney*, multi-award-winner *The Fastest Clock in the Universe, Ghost from a Perfect Place, Vincent River, Mercury Fur, Leaves of Glass, Piranha Heights, Tender Napalm* (London Fringe Best Play Award nominee), *Shivered* (OffWestEnd Best New Play Award nominee) and *Dark Vanilla Jungle* (*Scotsman* Fringe First winner), plus several plays for young people: *Karamazoo, Fairytaleheart, Moonfleece, Sparkleshark* and *Brokenville* (collectively known as *The Storyteller Sequence*), and a play for the whole family, *Feathers in the Snow*.

He has also written books for children, including *Scribbleboy* (shortlisted for the Carnegie Medal), *Kasper in the Glitter* (Whitbread Prize nominee), *Mighty Fizz Chilla* (shortlisted for the Blue Peter Book of the Year Award), *ZinderZunder, Vinegar Street, Zip's Apollo* and the bestseller *Krindlekrax* (Smarties Prize and WH Smith's Mind-Boggling Books Award winner), the stage play of which – adapted by Philip himself – premiered at Birmingham Rep in 2002.

He has directed three feature films from his own screenplays: *The Reflecting Skin* (winner of eleven international awards including the George Sadoul Prize), *The Passion of Darkly Noon* (winner of Best Director at the Porto Film Festival) and *Heartless* (winner of the Silver Méliès Award for Best Fantasy Film). For the latter two, Philip co-wrote several songs, of which 'Who Will Love Me Now?' (performed by PJ Harvey) was voted BBC Radio 1's Top Film Song of 1998 and was covered by the techno-house band Sunscreem (as 'Please Save Me'), becoming a club and viral hit.

In 2010 Philip, along with songwriting collaborator Nick Bicât, formed music group Dreamskin Cradle and their first album, *Songs from Grimm*, is available on iTunes, Amazon and all major download sites. Philip is also a performance artist in his own right, and his highly charged readings of his ongoing poetry sequence *Lovesongs for Extinct Creatures* have proved increasingly popular in recent years.

In 2012 *WhatsOnStage* named him as one of the Jubilee Playwrights (sixty of the most influential British writers to have emerged in the past six decades). Philip has won both the *Evening Standard*'s Most Promising Newcomer to British Film and Most Promising Playwright Awards, the only person ever to receive both prizes.

Gemma Whelan

Gemma is an actress and comedian, and in 2013 was nominated for the *Stage* Award for Best Solo Performance for the world premiere of Philip Ridley's *Dark Vanilla Jungle*, which subsequently toured and transferred to Soho Theatre.

Gemma is best known for TV roles including Yara Greyjoy in the hit HBO TV drama *Game of Thrones* and recently as Quaint Irene in the BBC's *Mapp and Lucia*. Forthcoming TV work includes *Cut* (Channel 4), *Uncle* and *Asylum* (both BBC). Other TV includes *Ruddy Hell, It's Harry and Paul* (BBC2), *Badults* (BBC Three), *Doctor Brown, The Persuasionists* (all Channel 4), *Threesome* (Comedy Central) and *Cardinal Burns* (E4).

Other theatre includes the leading role of Rachel Crabbe in the smash hit *One Man, Two Guvnors* (West End). Film includes *Gulliver's Travels*, *The Wolfman*, *Magnificent Strangers* and *Madness of the Dance*.

As a comedian she won a Funny Women Award in 2010 and has appeared at the Edinburgh Festival in solo character comedy show *Chastity Butterworth & the Spanish Hamster* (Assembly) and on the BBC's *Live at the Electric*.

Sean Michael Verey

Sean is Bristol born and probably best known for playing the lead role of Jamie Prince in hit BBC Three sitcom *Pramface*. He also has appeared in TV shows such as *Skins* (Channel 4), *Holby City* (BBC), TV film *The Kindness of Strangers* (ITV) and feature film *Nina Forever*, due to be released in 2015.

Sean starred in the original cast of Phillip Ridley's play *Moonfleece* (Riverside Studios and UK tour) in 2010, directed by David Mercatali; and he recently toured the UK with the *Birds of a Feather* stage show.

Amanda Daniels

Amanda has previously worked with playwright Philip Ridley on the world premiere of his play *Shivered* (Southwark Playhouse). In 2005 she won the Edinburgh Fringe Award for Best Actress for *Third Finger, Left Hand* (York Theatre Royal, New End Theatre, Assembly Rooms), which also transferred to Trafalgar Studios 2.

Other theatre credits include *Wild Horses* (Theatre503), *Days of Significance*, *The Winter's Tale*, *Pericles* (all RSC), *13 Grape Street* (Pleasance Theatre), *Tartuffe* (Cockpit Theatre), *The Accrington Pals* (Pentameters), *April in Paris* (Man in the Moon) and *A Midsummer Night's Dream* (Grange Court).

Television includes *Call the Midwife*, *EastEnders*, *Silent Witness*, *Holby City*, *Doctors*, *Casualty*, *Sea of Souls*, *Auf Wiedersehen, Pet* (all BBC), *Doc Martin*, *The Bill*, *Rosemary & Thyme* (all ITV) and *Marital Harmony* (pilot).

Film includes *Balloon Man*, *Paroxetine* and *A Woman Spawned*.

David Mercatali

David is a director and writer based in London, currently Associate Director at Southwark Playhouse. This is his fifth Philip Ridley premiere, following the acclaimed and controversial *Moonfleece* (Riverside Studios and UK tour), the widely celebrated *Tender Napalm* (Southwark Playhouse and UK tour), hit family show *Feathers in the Snow* (Southwark Playhouse) and Fringe First winner *Dark Vanilla Jungle* (Pleasance Edinburgh, UK Tour and Soho Theatre).

Other recent credits include world premieres of Alice Birch's *Little Light* (Orange Tree Theatre), Anders Lustgarten's *Black Jesus* (Finborough), *Johnny Got His Gun* (Southwark Playhouse and UK tour), Papatango Prize winner *Coolatully* (Finborough), Timberlake Wertenbaker's *Our Ajax* (Southwark Playhouse), *Sochi 2014* (Hope Theatre), verbatim drama *Someone to Blame* (King's Head Theatre), *Weights* (Blue Elephant), *Runners: The Return* (Underbelly) and *People's Day* (Pleasance Islington).

David was nominated for the 2011 *Evening Standard* Outstanding Newcomer and OffWestEnd Best Director Award for *Tender Napalm*. He has developed work at Paines Plough, the Finborough and Theatre503. His first play, *The Sound*, premiered in 2009 at the Blue Elephant Theatre.

William Reynolds

William Reynolds trained at the Motley Theatre Design School. He previously designed premieres of Ridley's plays *Moonfleece*, *Tender Napalm* and *Dark Vanilla Jungle*, all with director David Mercatali.

Recent lighting designs include: *Peter Pan and The Designers of the Caribbean* (Bloomsbury), *Alice* (UK tour), *The Two Worlds of Charlie F* (Theatre Royal Haymarket and international tour), *Bee Detective* (UK tour), *The Magic Flute* (Palestine tour).

Recent set and lighting designs include *Well* (Theatre Royal Bury St Edmunds), *Arab Nights* (UK tour), *Waiting* and *Sexing the Cherry* (Southbank Centre).

Projection designs include *Rites of War* (Stratford Circus and UK tour), *Flicker* (Sadler's Wells), *La Cenerentola* (Bury Court Opera), *Twelfth Night* (UK Tour), *The Gambler* (Royal Opera), *La Bohème* (Palestine tour) and *Das Rhinegold* (National Resisopera).

Hannah Hauer-King

Hannah graduated from Georgetown University with a BA in Theatrical Studies and was recently resident as Assistant Director at Soho Theatre. Directing credits include *Pool (No Water)*, *Waiting for Phillip Glass*, *Spring Awakening*, *Spike Heels*, *Unf**king Believable* and rehearsed readings of *Dry Land* and *A Dramatic Night.* Assistant directing includes *Daytona* (Park Theatre), *Symphony*, *I Kiss Your Heart* (both Soho Theatre), *Hamlet* (Georgetown University), *The Deep Blue Sea* and *References to Salvador Dali Make Me Hot* (both Nomadic Theatre).

Metal Rabbit Productions

Metal Rabbit was established in 2012 by producers George Warren and Martha Rose Wilson. Their first production was *Fiesta: The Sun Also Rises*, a new adaptation from Ernest Hemingway written and directed by Alex Helfrecht, which enjoyed a sold-out run at Trafalgar Studios in February 2013.

Other recent productions include the UK premiere of Dalton Trumbo's *Johnny Got His Gun* (Southwark Playhouse and UK tour), nominated for four Off West End Awards including Best Director (David Mercatali); and two projects at the Old Red Lion Theatre, Neil Bartlett's adaptation of *A Christmas Carol* and the world premiere of *Lardo* by Mike Stone.

For more information, visit www.metalrabbitproductions.com

Supporting Wall

Producing company Supporting Wall was founded in 2008 by Ben Monks and Will Young. *Radiant Vermin* is their fourth collaboration with Philip Ridley, following world premieres of Fringe First winner *Dark Vanilla Jungle* at Pleasance Edinburgh, on tour and at Soho Theatre; the smash hit Southwark Playhouse run and subsequent UK tour of *Tender Napalm*; and their acclaimed and controversial professional premiere of *Moonfleece*, in London and on UK tour in the run-up to the 2010 general election.

Other recent productions include the London premiere of Mike Bartlett's TMA Award-winning play *Bull* (Young Vic); world premieres of Olivier Award-winner Timberlake Wertenbaker's *Our Ajax* (Southwark Playhouse) and Chris Lee's social work drama *Shallow Slumber* (Soho Theatre); Danny Saleeb's chamber opera *Yellow* (Tête à Tête: The Opera Festival); JMK Award-winner *The Jewish Wife* (Battersea Arts Centre); and rapid-response political theatre event *Election Drama* (New Players Theatre), described by the *New Statesman* as 'a breathtaking feat of theatrical chutzpah'.

Ben and Will were nominated for the OffWestEnd 'Offie' Best Producer Award in both 2011 and 2012. Supporting Wall has also managed and promoted UK and international tours and festivals for a range of clients across theatre, dance, comedy, film and festivals.

Supporting Wall Limited is a not for profit company registered in England and Wales, number 7081594. For more information, visit www.supportingwall.com.

Radiant Vermin

Find out what you're afraid of and go live there
Chuck Palanich

Babies are the enemy of the human race
Isaac Asimov

Horror is the removal of masks
Robert Bloch

Characters

Jill
Ollie
Miss Dee

Ollie *and* **Jill**, *late twenties.*

Jill *is holding a baby.*

Jill   Hello, I'm Jill.

Ollie   And I'm Ollie.

Jill   This is our son Benjy.

Ollie   We'd like to tell you about our home.

Jill   Our *dream* home.

Ollie   That's right.

Jill   *How* we got it.

Ollie   Exactly. Because . . . well . . .

Jill   We're good people.

Ollie   We *hope* we are.

Jill   We *try* to be.

Ollie   And yet . . . *some* of the things we've done –

Jill   To *get* our dream home.

Ollie   Well . . . they're not exactly . . . nice.

Jill   No, they're not.

Ollie   In fact they're . . .

Jill   They're . . .

Ollie   . . . Horrible.

Jill   I'm afraid they are, yes.

Ollie   Some might even say . . . shocking.

Jill   They would.

Ollie   But I'm sure –

Jill   We're *both* sure.

Ollie   Once we've . . . explained –

Jill   *Why* we did –

Ollie   *What* we did –

Jill   Then you'll understand.

Ollie   Because *everything* we did.

Jill   No matter how horrible.

Ollie   No matter how shocking.

Jill   We did it all –

Ollie and **Jill**   For baby.

Jill   Talking of which – Look at him!

Ollie   He's out to the world.

Jill   He's had a busy day.

Ollie   His birthday.

Jill   We had a party.

Ollie   The birthday party from hell.

Jill   Don't give away the end of the –

Ollie   Sorry, sorry.

Jill   They're all be waiting for the birthday party from hell how!

Ollie   They won't, they won't – Birthday party! Forget I said it – See?

Jill   . . . I'll just pop Benjy in his cot.

Ollie   I'll be getting things started, shall I?

Jill   Yes, yes, I won't be long.

Exits.

Ollie Right! Now me and Jill – we've talked about where to begin explaining all this. And we've decided to start one and a half years ago. That's six months before Benjamin was born. So. We're not in our dream home now. Oh, no. We've in a tiny flat in a place called Red Ocean Estate – Oh! You've heard of it, I see. Saw the documentary on telly, did you? Crime capital of the universe and all that. Honestly, you'd think everyone on the estate was either a drug dealer or suicidal. True, the Russian family that gassed themselves *were* drug dealers, but to spend half the programme on that single event was misleading in the extreme if you want my opinion. So . . . here I am! In our Red Ocean Estate flat. Laying some more mice traps!

Jill *returns*.

Jill We've just got a letter.

Ollie Too late for the post.

Jill Hand delivered. Looks official. (*Reading*.) 'Dear Mr and Mrs Swift, please allow me to introduce myself. My name is Miss Dee and I would like – with your permission, of course – to talk to you about a subject that is very close to my heart. Namely, dream homes.'

Ollie Dream homes?

Jill 'I have been asked by the local council to head a new department that will function as an offshoot of the government's housing programme. The name of this new department is the D.S.R.C.D.H. Otherwise known as the Department of Social Regeneration through the Creation of Dream Homes.'

Ollie Never heard of it.

Jill 'It gives me the deepest joy to inform both of you that you've been selected for participation in our new scheme.'

Ollie What scheme?

Jill 'To put it simply. We will give you a house.'

Ollie   *What*?!

Jill   'I repeat: we will give you a house.'

Ollie   What's the – ?

Jill   'What's the catch, I hear you asking. So let me – Miss Dee – be totally upfront. The house will not necessarily be in the best state of repair nor will it necessarily be in a prime location.'

Ollie   A slum in the –

Jill   'Before you say, "A slum in the sticks –"'

Ollie   No way.

Takes letter.

'Before you say, "A slum in the sticks", let me assure you this is not the case. I give you my world it will be a property that has much potential in a locale that has much potential. If you want to hear more about this wonderful opportunity please meet me at the house in question tomorrow at midday. The address is below along with directions how to get there.' – Oh, it's a joke!

She takes letter back.

Jill   'I will have the contract and the keys and, if you want to take possession, you can do so immediately. Please, children –'

Ollie   Children?!

Jill   '– don't let this wonderful opportunity slip through your fingers. Best Wishes. Miss Dee.'

Ollie   It's a scam!

Jill   I don't know . . .

Ollie   It's a pathetic telly show or something. We'll go there and they'll film us getting all excited. You know? Let's make fun of the underclass desperate to get on the property ladder.

Jill   We are *not* 'the underclass'.

Ollie   Okay, okay.

Jill   Desperate, possibly. Underclass? No.

Ollie   It could be a gang. You thought of that? We'll be robbed at gun point.

Jill   Robbed of *what*? We haven't *got* anything.

Ollie   What about the car?

Jill   The *car*?! I feel sorry for anyone who wants *that*.

Ollie   It's perfectly serviceable – What're you looking for?

Jill   We've got other letters from the town hall somewhere.

Ollie   What's that going to prove?

Jill   I just want to check . . . Aha! Look! Same letterhead. Phone number.

Ollie   Any joker can get those – Don't tell me you're ringing them?!

Jill   Why not?

Ollie   They'll *laugh* at you.

Jill   What if they do? At least we'll know if – Oh, good afternoon. My name's Jillian Swift. I'm so sorry to bother you but I've just received a letter and it *says* it's from you but it's a very odd letter and so – Yes, that's right . . . Oh, I see . . . I see . . . I see . . . Thank you.

Hangs up.

Ollie   Well?

Jill   Perfectly legitimate.

Ollie   No!

Jill   Miss Dee doesn't have an actual office in the town hall but she'll give us her phone number when we meet her tomorrow.

Ollie   . . . I'm still not sure . . .

Jill   What have we got to lose?

He doesn't answer.

Ollie! If you do not agree to see this house then I will get very upset. And if I get very upset our unborn baby will get very upset. And you remember what that psychiatrist on telly said about pregnancy shaping the rest of a child's life. Do you want our child to grow into someone who machine guns his classmates?

Slight pause.

Ollie   It's the next day.

Jill   We're driving to the house.

Ollie   We turn right . . . Here?

Jill   Yes. Then straight on to the roundabout – Oh, look, Ollie. The old car plant.

Ollie   What's left of it.

Jill   Look at all those weeds.

Ollie   Know what it reminds me of? Those Malayan temples they found in that jungle. They sacrificed hundred and hundreds of –

Jill   Roundabout!

Ollie   What exit do we – ?

Jill   Second! . . . And we need the third turning – no, *fourth*! – on the right. Gilead Close should be at the end.

Ollie   Jesus. Nothing but deserted streets. Not a soul.

Jill   What's that saying you're so fond of? 'Hell is other people'?

Ollie   I'm not sure it applies in these circumstances. Also, there's a debate about what Jean-Paul Sartre exactly meant by that. There's some that think he was referring to –

Jill   Ollie.

Ollie   Sorry.

Jill   . . . The houses look solid enough.

Ollie   The houses in Chernobyl look solid enough but I wouldn't want to –

Jill   Turn!

Ollie   Left?

Jill   Right! – What's that noise?

Ollie   The exhaust's hit something.

Jill   It's not going to fall off, is it?

Ollie   It should be fine.

Jill   That doesn't fill me with confidence, Ollie.

Ollie   Gilead Close! – What number do we – ?

Jill   Three.

Ollie   I . . . I can't make out the numbers.

Jill   Well, there're five houses in all.

Ollie   So three should be –

Jill   Middle one – Here! Stop!

The car stops.

Slight pause.

Ollie   Chernobyl chic.

Jill   If you make one more reference to that God-awful place –

Ollie   Alright, alright.

Jill   . . . Well, we won't see much from inside the car, will we.

They get out of car.

Jill   . . . Doesn't seem to be any sign of Miss Dee.

Ollie   We're a bit early.

Jill   The front of the house looks okay.

Ollie   The garage is a write-off.

Jill   It matches our car, then, doesn't it.

Ollie   At least our car has doors! – Where're you going?

Jill   Looking through the windows.

Ollie   Careful, Jill!

Jill   Big rooms.

Ollie   Big decorating.

Jill   The front door's open! – Miss Dee?! . . . Miss Dee?!

Ollie   You're not going inside?

Jill   Why not?

Ollie   I think we should wait for – ?

Jill   Ollie!

He joins her.

Oh, the hallway's lovely.

Ollie   If you like the smell of damp.

Jill   Two reception rooms. We can knock that wall down. More open plan.

Ollie Am I the only one who can see loose wires everywhere? – Where you going now?

Jill The kitchen's huge! You know what would look perfect here. Those units we saw at Selfridges. The peach and white. Remember?

Ollie I remember the price tag.

Jill We can save for it.

Ollie If we both work till we're a hundred and fifty, sure.

Jill Let's go upstairs.

Ollie I'm sure we should wait for –

Jill Ollie!

He joins her.

. . . Three bedrooms. *Three*!

Ollie Yes, yes, I can count.

Jill This'll be ours . . . And that – that can be a room for guests.

Ollie We've *never* had guests.

Jill Well, we will when we've got somewhere to put them, won't we. And this room here – oh, this would make the *perfect* nursery, wouldn't it?

Ollie If we can get Mary Poppins to clean it, sure.

Miss Dee There you are, children!

Miss Dee *has appeared.*

Jill Oh! . . . Miss Dee?

Miss Dee Miss Dee – that's me! What a joy to meet you at last.

Ollie *and* **Jill** *go to shake hands.*

Miss Dee   No, no, give Miss Dee a hug like the old friends I feel we all are.

They hug.

Is that a new dress, Jillian?

Jill   What – ? Oh. Yes. The baby's beginning to show – It's not too frumpy, is it?

Miss Dee   Certainly not. It's delightful – Don't you think so, Oliver?

Ollie   Er . . . yes – Have we been under surveillance?

Miss Dee   What on earth makes you say that?

Ollie   You seem strangely au fait with my wife's wardrobe.

Miss Dee   Miss Dee knows what Miss Dee knows.

Jill   Miss Dee . . . this house –

Miss Dee   The contract's in my bag!

Ollie   I have some questions first.

Miss Dee   Why were *you* chosen?

Ollie   . . . That's one, yes.

Miss Dee   Because you're the correct choice.

Ollie   What's that supposed to – ?

Miss Dee   You are a maker of things, Oliver. A craftsman. Those shelves you put up in your flat? Beautiful. The tiling in the bathroom? No professional could've done it better.

Jill   He's so good with his hands.

Miss Dee   Oh, he is. Very good. The trouble is he has no taste.

Jill   Oh, that's not fair, Miss Dee.

Miss Dee   But it is true, my dear. And you know it. Fortunately, you *do* have taste. Oodles of it. The way you designed your bedroom? I've rarely seen such a masterful sense of colour. And the choice of curtains, rug, ornaments – Perfection. Pure perfection. You – (*Pointing at* **Jill**.) – know the *what*, but not the *how*. You – (*Pointing at* **Ollie**.) – know the *how*, but not the *what*. Together, you're a marriage made in heaven – Contract!

Gives contract to **Ollie**.

Ollie   So . . . we just get *given* it. This house.

Miss Dee   Clause One, as you see.

Ollie   And it's ours. One hundred per cent.

Miss Dee   Yes.

Ollie   You can't take it back?

Miss Dee   No.

Ollie   Not ever? We can pass it on to our children?

Miss Dee   No. Yes.

Ollie   And if we sell it?

Miss Dee   Clause Two.

Ollie   . . . We keep all the money.

Miss Dee   Every penny.

Jill   Oh, Ollie, it's too good to be true.

Ollie   Dad used to say if something's too good to be true it usually is.

Jill   You're determined to see problems.

Ollie   I'm determined we make the right decision.

Jill   And I'm *not*?!

Miss Dee   Children, children, please. Listen to your Miss Dee. This house is a wonderful chance for you both. It's one of those moments that – if you let it slip through your fingers – you'll always be wondering 'what if?' And believe me there's nothing worse than life's 'what ifs'. So please, I *beg* of you. Accept this house. Because I tell you – as God is my witness – no two people are more deserving.

Jill   Oh, surely . . . surely not – Ollie?

Ollie   Were nothing special.

Miss Dee   Nothing spec – Jillian! Your mother! Those afternoon church tea parties she organised for slobbering geriatrics. Who was it made the sandwiches and cakes? Who set out the tables with all those folded napkins so delicate and delightful? Who did all that, child?

Jill   . . . I did.

Miss Dee   And when your mum's arthritis got so bad her hands swelled up like rubber gloves full of golf balls – Who was it washed her? Who was it dressed her, fed her and – forgive any inappropriate language – took her to the toilet and cleaned her where the sun don't shine? Who did that?

Jill   *Any* daughter would have done the same.

Miss Dee   No, child. They would not – And you, Oliver! Living with your dad's alcoholism wasn't easy, was it? All hugs and kisses one second, then a Babycham too many and – Bahm!

Ollie   Dad was *never* violent.

Miss Dee   Not physically. But verbally? His words would slap you and lash you. Yet you never retaliated. Not once – our husband's a good man, Jill. You're *both* good people.

Ollie   Yes, yes, all very flattering I'm sure but –

Miss Dee   You want to know what the government gets out of all this.

Ollie   Yes.

Miss Dee   How to explain – ? . . . Tell me, have you ever heard about the Amazonian jungle plant *Lux Lucis Atrum Nex Nemus* commonly known as the 'Shimmering Glimmering Tree'?

Jill   Er . . . no – Ollie?

Ollie   Never.

Miss Dee   Oh, it's very rare. I myself have only seen one example. An old woman I knew when I was a child – indeed the woman who taught me most of what I know today – she had one. 'I want to show you the most beautiful tree in the world,' she said to me one day. She took me into her garden. 'There!' I have to admit, what I saw did not impress. Its leaves were dark green – black almost – and it was covered with dull fruits the size of a baby's eyeballs. But then the woman took the hem of her apron and polished one of the fruits. Polished till it sparkled. The next thing I see . . . the fruit next to it starts to sparkle. All by itself. No polishing needed. And then the fruit next to that. And the fruit next to that. Until the whole tree – oh, it sparkles like treasure!

Ollie   So you're saying . . . if we renovate this house –

Miss Dee   Other people will see it and think . . .?

Jill   I can do the same to the house next door!

Miss Dee   And the house next to that.

Jill   Until the whole Close sparkles.

Miss Dee   Oh, more! The streets all round!

Jill   The whole area?

Miss Dee   Of course! Regeneration through –

Jill   – the Creation of Dream Homes.

Miss Dee   All it needs is for one house to sparkle.

Jill   Oh, it makes sense, Ollie.

Ollie   It makes sense if it *works*.

Miss Dee   It *always* works.

Ollie   You've done this before?

Miss Dee   Many times.

Ollie   And it's always successful?

Miss Dee   If I've chosen the clients correctly, yes.

Jill   Give me that contract!

Snatches contract from **Miss Dee***.*

Ollie   What the – ?

Jill *signs contract.*

Ollie   Jill! Jesus! Wh-what've you done?!

Jill   I want this house.

Ollie   I'm *part* of this equation too, you know.

Miss Dee   The contract needs *both* your signatures.

Ollie   There! We *both* need to . . . to –

Miss Dee   Consult!

Ollie   Exactly! We need to *consult* about things.

Takes contract from **Jill.**

Jill   *What* things?

Miss Dee   He's worried about all the red tape involved –
Right?

Ollie   That's on my mind, yes.

Miss Dee   Fear not. Clause Four. You see? We will arrange
all the legals. We will transfer all utility bills on your behalf.
You will have no forms to fill in or phone calls to make.

Ollie   But what about – ?

Miss Dee   Informing your doctor, your dentist, finding new
surgeries – Everything done for you.

Ollie   And the – ?

Miss Dee   Getting your furniture here? We will arrange for a delivery van. And workmen. As many as you need. They will take away the rubbish from this house. They will bring anything you want from your flat to here. And before you ask – Clause Five, subsection B – it won't cost you a penny. You see?

Jill   Oh, Ollie, sign. *Sign!*

Ollie   Wait, wait . . . What's this? Clause Six, subsection six.

Miss Dee   'The signatories must maintain discretion.'

Ollie   What's *that* supposed to mean?

Miss Dee   What do you *think* it means?

Jill   . . .We mustn't attract attention. Getting a house for free. People can get jealous – Right, Miss Dee?

Miss Dee   You want to be on good terms with your neighbours.

Ollie   Okay, okay. What about basic improvements?

Miss Dee   All repairs and renovations to the property are your responsibility.

Ollie   Aha!

Jill   But . . . but surely that's fair.

Miss Dee   The basic structure of the house is sound.

Ollie   The whole place needs re-wiring.

Miss Dee   That would be advisable, yes.

Jill   So . . . how long will that take?

Miss Dee   One week.

Ollie   If you're a professional.

Jill   Then we'll *get* a professional.

Ollie   We can't *afford* a professional.

Miss Dee   I'm sure you're more than capable, Oliver. Say it takes *longer* than a week. You can have candles for light. A small gas heater for cooking. As for heating . . . well, the weather's clement.

Jill   We won't freeze.

Miss Dee   You won't.

Ollie   What about hot water?

Jill   There's no hot water?!

Ollie   Ha! She hadn't thought of that.

Jill   I don't care! I'll wash at the sink!

Ollie   She says that *now*.

Jill   Ollie. This is a chance for us. *Please*.

Ollie   . . . I'm not sure.

Jill   He's not sure! He's never bloody sure. One day he'll drop dead and you know what they'll write on his tombstone? 'Here lies Oliver Swift . . . but he's still not bloody sure.'

Slight pause.

Ollie *heads for door.*

Jill   Where're you going?

Ollie   To check the exhaust on the car.

Jill   Oh, Ollie –

Ollie *exits.*

Miss Dee   Let him go, child.

Jill   . . . I shouldn't have said what I did, Miss Dee.

Miss Dee   . . . Where did you both meet?

Jill   What – ? Oh! The local church. Mum was helping Father Vianney put on a party for some underprivileged kids and – I have a feeling you know this already.

Miss Dee   I'd still like to hear it from your lips.

Jill   Mum had booked a magician. Mr Mysterio the Mysterious. He was late. The party was almost over when his van rolled up. I was outside waiting for it. A spotty teenager wearing glasses gets out.

Miss Dee   Oliver.

Jill   'Sorry, sorry,' he said. 'We've been stuck in traffic.' Mr Mysterio was Ollie's dad. Ollie – he was the assistant in the act. He did all these funny voices to distract the children. You should have seen the children, Miss Dee. They couldn't stop laughing. And Mr Mysterio – oh, he had a magic wand that shot sparks out of the end – Whoosh!

Miss Dee   Impressive.

Jill   Ollie made it! And lots of the other things too. After the show me and Ollie talked and talked. We were so . . . open with each other. Right from the start. He told me he wasn't religious but he was in the school choir. I said I was too. And by the end of that very first conversation . . . we . . .

Miss Dee   You were in love.

Jill   Oh, Miss Dee! He's beeping the hooter. I'll . . . I'll have to go. You understand, don't you?

Miss Dee   Of course.

Jill   Thank you for . . . for thinking of us . . . for this. Perhaps . . . sometime in the future. . .

Miss Dee   Perhaps . . .

Jill *goes to leave –*

Miss Dee   Just one last thing – Oh, I know it's going to sound foolish and you'll probably think me a silly old woman –

Jill   What is it, Miss Dee?

Miss Dee   . . . Selfridges.

Jill   Selfridges?

Miss Dee   It's my favourite department store in the whole world and . . . well, I know you went there last week.

Jill   That's right.

Miss Dee   I haven't been there for years. Will you tell me about your trip? What you saw. The colours. The smells – Is there still an angel over the entrance?

Jill   Yes! Yes, there is!

Miss Dee   And when you go through the revolving doors – Perfume!

Jill   Oh, the smell made me giddy.

Miss Dee   And all those magical names – Shalimar.

Jill   Estée Lauder.

Miss Dee   Dior.

Jill   Yves St Laurent.

Miss Dee   You took the escalators up?

Jill   Up and down, up and down.

Miss Dee   What things caught your eye?

Jill   What *didn't*? I wanted it *all* – There's the hooter again!

Miss Dee   And then? You went back to your flat?

Jill   What – ? Oh. Yes.

Miss Dee   And how did that make you feel?

Jill   . . . Abandoned. Oh, I know that sounds over the top. And . . . well, how can I be abandoned? They say God's everywhere, don't they.

Miss Dee   They do.

Jill   Well, there's a place he doesn't visit very often. And that's Red Ocean Estate.

Ollie *has appeared (unseen by* **Jill***).*

Jill   It sucks all the joy out of you, that place. All the . . . the – Hope! That's it. There's no hope. I don't want to bring our baby into a world like that. What will its future be? Drugs? Gangs? Prison? I want *more* than that for our child. I want . . . this house. Oh, yes, I know there'll be problems. Ollie's right. He usually is. But . . . but at least we'll have . . . we'll have the *hope* of things getting better. That's all I want. Isn't that the least we owe our child? Hope.

Slight pause.

Ollie *signs contract.*

Miss Dee   Enjoy your new home.

Heads for door.

Ollie   Oh! Your phone number, Miss Dee.

Miss Dee   Eh? What's that?

Ollie   The town hall said you'd give us your phone number.

Miss Dee   Why on earth would they say that?

Ollie   If we need to contact you?

Miss Dee   If *you* need to contact *me*, *I* will contact *you*.

Leaves.

Jill   It's the next day.

Ollie   We've moved out of the flat.

Jill   And we're in our house – The removal men were a godsend.

Ollie   Should've seen this one bossing them around.

Jill   Well, *some*body had to get things organised.

Ollie   You were magnificent, sweetheart.

Jill   One of them said he could do the re-wiring.

Ollie   *I'm* doing that.

Jill   He can do it quickly.

Ollie   I can do it cheaper.

Jill   I want a hot bath, Ollie!

Ollie   What did I tell you? Eh?

Jill   I'm pregnant! I need hygiene!

Ollie   I'll start work first thing tomorrow. You'll be having a nice hot soak by –

Jill   Tomorrow night?

Ollie   . . . The day after.

Jill   Promise?

Ollie   Promise – Bedtime?

Jill   Let's light the candles.

Ollie   We've bought three big boxes.

Jill   D'you like our candlesticks?

Ollie   A wedding present.

Jill   From Father Vianney. Solid brass.

Ollie   He stole them from the church, I think.

Jill   Ollie!

Ollie   Sorry, sorry. But they *are* a bit . . . Gothic.

Jill   Art nouveau – Window!

Ollie   Eh?

Jill   We haven't put a curtain up.

Ollie   There's no neighbours, Jill.

Jill   I know that but . . . oh, it don't feel right.

Ollie   Okay, okay. I'll hang a sheet over it.

Jill   Thank you.

Ollie   Can't have you refusing to take your clothes off, can we. Not when I'm in dire need of some frivolous and hopefully indecent fondling.

Jill   Ollie! Don't!

Ollie   I'm trying to be erotic.

Jill   I know, sweetheart, I know. But . . . not in *front* of everyone.

Ollie   Oh! Sorry – Sorry! – Hang on! What's that?

Jill   What's *what*?

Ollie   Other side of the waste ground.

She goes to him.

Jill   I can't see . . .

Ollie   There!

Jill   Oh! A bonfire.

Ollie   There's another over there.

Jill   Who's made them, d'you think?

Ollie   The homeless. Didn't you see them under the flyover?

Jill   No.

Ollie   Cardboard city.

Jill   Oh, Ollie . . . Put the sheet up! Quick!

Ollie   Don't worry. They're too far away to see us.

Jill   If *we* can see *their* fire, I'm sure *they* can see *our* candles.

Ollie   . . . Next night!

Jill   We're asleep in bed!

Slight pause.

What's that?

Ollie   Eh . . .?

Jill   A noise.

Ollie   Where?

Jill   Downstairs.

Ollie   What sort of – ?

Jill   Shhh!

Slight pause.

There!

Ollie   It's coming from the kitchen.

Jill   Did you lock the back door?

Ollie   I thought *you* did!

Slight pause.

Jill   There it is again!

Ollie   Probably a fox.

Jill   You think so?

Ollie   It can smell the food. It'll rummage around a bit and then just . . .

Jill   'Then just?'

Ollie   . . . Go away.

Slight pause.

Okay. That's no fox.

Jill   You can't be sure.

Ollie   I can.

Jill   But how – ?

Ollie Jill! What's down there is opening and closing cupboard doors. Now, unless it happens to be a fox genetically engineered by Pixar, I suggest it is *not* a fox.

Jill Oh, Ollie.

Ollie I'm calling the police.

Jill It'll take them ages to get here.

Ollie What else do you suggest we –? Shit!

Jill What?

Ollie No signal – Try yours.

Jill . . . No signal.

Ollie Shit!

Jill It's one of the homeless.

Ollie What?

Jill Downstairs. They saw our candles.

Ollie Well, if it is . . . they'll probably have a bite to eat, then go.

Jill '*Probably* have a bite to eat, then go'?

Ollie If they wanted to hurt us they'd've done it by now.

Jill Perhaps they need to get their strength up first.

Ollie Why must you be so negative all the time?

Jill *Me* negative?!

Ollie I have more faith in human nature than you.

Jill So . . . we just wait here like nothing's happening?

Ollie . . . Yes.

Slight pause.

Jill I am more than a little stressed, Ollie.

Ollie   . . . Perhaps I should call out.

Jill   'Call out'?

Ollie   Let them know we know.

Jill   What good'll *that* do?

Ollie   Scare them off.

Jill   What if it sends them up here with a carving knife.

Ollie   There you go with that negativity again!

Jill   If you say that one more time I'll – What're you doing?

Ollie   What's it look like?

Jill   You're not going downstairs!?

Ollie   You and baby are getting stressed.

Jill   There might be more than one down there, Ollie.

Ollie   Then I'll . . .

Jill   What?

Ollie   Politely ask them to leave.

Jill   '*Politely* ask them'?!

Ollie   They're just homeless, Jill. Not psycho killers.

Jill   What you looking for?

Ollie   A weapon.

Jill   I thought you just said –

Ollie   A precaution. That's all.

Jill   Listen. I think we should just stay up here and –

Ollie   No. If we let them get away with it tonight there might be a whole army of them tomorrow. We'll be a . . . an open bloody house for every passing vagrant who – Candlestick! This'll crack a skull in.

Jill   I'm scared.

Ollie   Me too. Stay here. Okay? . . . *Jill*?

Jill   Okay, okay.

Ollie   I'm leaving the bedroom now . . . I'm at the top of stairs . . . 'Hello? Anyone there?' . . . I'm going down the stairs . . . I'm at the bottom . . . 'I warn you! I'm armed!'

Jill   What can you see?

Ollie   The kitchen door's closed.

Jill   Can you hear anything?

Ollie   . . . No. Stay up there.

Jill   Say you've got a gun.

Ollie   'I've got a gun!' . . . I'm walking down the corridor now. I'm pushing the kitchen door open. I'm going into the kitchen. 'I don't want any trouble.' The back door is open. Food on the floor. I keep expecting to see a face but . . . nothing – AHHH! Someone's grabbed me from behind!

Jill   Ollie!

Ollie   Hot breath down my neck. Fingers are around my neck. I kick. Force myself back . . . back . . . I crash whoever's grabbing me into the sink. The grip loosens. I turn. It's a man. He's got a grey beard. He snatches something from the draining board. I think it's a knife. He lashes at me. I swing the candlestick. I catch his upper arm. He lets out a cry but it doesn't stop him grabbing my hair. He raises his other hand – The knife! I drop the candlestick and catch hold of his wrist. The blade's getting closer and closer. 'Please . . . Just go! I don't . . . I don't want to hurt you.' He's not listening. I knee him in the stomach and shove as hard as I can. He stumbles back. He slips on something. He crashes against the kitchen door.

Jill   Ollie!

Ollie   He's just standing there. He's not moving. His eyes are wide. Then I see . . . dangling from his overcoat pocket . . . hearing aids. Why wasn't he wearing them? Perhaps they're broken. 'I am ver-ry sor-ry. I must have scared you when I –' Is that blood dripping from his hands . . . pooling at his feet . . . Oh, God! The coat hook. On the back of the door . . .

Jill   Ollie!

Ollie   I pull the door open and go into the hall.

Jill   What's going on?

Ollie   I told you to stay upstairs!

Jill   Is that blood!

Ollie   Where?

Jill   There.

Ollie   It's . . . it's not mine.

Jill   Not . . .?

Ollie   We . . . we struggled . . . he stumbled.

Jill   Stumbled?

Ollie   Against the door . . . The coat hook . . .

Slight pause.

Jill *cries out.*

Jill   He's dead?!

Ollie   Calm down.

Jill   *'Calm down'*?! You've just killed a – *'Calm down'*?!

Ollie   Sit on the stairs.

Jill   I don't want to sit on the – Oh, God! God!

Ollie   Listen to me, Jill. You need to get a grip. The baby, Jill . . . *Jill*!

Jill   Okay . . . Okay . . .

Ollie   Deep breaths.

She breathes deep.

Ollie   . . . Now . . . what's happened here is just a . . . a bit of bad luck and –

Jill   . . . Look!

Ollie   Eh?

Jill   There! Under the kitchen door.

Ollie   Light?!

Jill   It so bright!

Ollie   Too bright to look at.

Jill   There's no electric, Ollie.

Ollie   I know that.

Jill   So what's causing the – ?

Ollie   I don't bloody know!

Jill   A searchlight! Helicopter?

Ollie   I can't hear any –

Jill   I want to know what it *is*, Ollie! I want to know right *now*!

Ollie   Shush, shush – Look. I think the light is –

Jill   It's fading.

Ollie   . . . Yes.

Jill   . . . It's gone.

Slight pause.

Ollie   Wait here . . .

Jill   Don't!

Ollie   I've got to find out –

Jill   No!

He stands still

Slight pause.

Jill   Well . . . take a quick look.

He approaches kitchen.

She starts murmuring a prayer.

Ollie   I push open the kitchen door . . .

Her praying gets louder.

He stares and –

Ollie   God . . .

Jill   . . . What?

Ollie   The body . . .

Jill   What about it? . . . Ollie?!

Ollie   It's gone.

Jill   Wh-what do you mean 'gone'?

Ollie   I mean it was here but now it's . . . oh, fuck!

Jill   What, Ollie?

Ollie   Oh. Fuck.

Slight pause.

She joins him and –

She screams. Then –

Jill   It's the kitchen we saw in Selfridges!

Ollie   It's wonderful!

Jill   '*Wonderful*!' Is that all you can say?

Ollie   But it *is*.

Jill   But how . . . *how* . . .?

Ollie   I don't know.

Jill   . . . Oh, you know. *You* know!

Ollie   *What*?!

Jill   I'm not a *complete* fool.

Ollie   Jill, I don't understand what you're –

Jill   This is one of your tricks.

Ollie   Of course it's bloody not

Jill   It *has* to be.

Ollie   Jill. It is *not* me.

Jill   Well it's . . . it's *some*thing.

Ollie   It's *some*thing, yes. But it's *not* me.

Jill   . . . A film crew! You *said* it would happen. Didn't you? Eh?

Ollie   I *know* I did but –

Jill   I bet there's cameras everywhere. They're laughing at us right now – Okay! Desperate underclass humiliated! Ha, ha! Game over.

Ollie   Jill!

Jill   Show yourselves!

Ollie   *Jill*! It is *not* a bloody telly programme!

Jill   It *has* to be!

Ollie   Listen! There was a man . . . hanging from a –

Jill   An actor!

Ollie   He was *dead*.

Jill   A *good* actor.

Ollie   Jesus Christ! There was a three-inch hook in his fucking skull, Jill! I stared into his eyes. Dead eyes. You hear me? Dead! *Dead!*

Jill   . . . We've got to get out of here!

Ollie   Stop!

Jill   We've got to . . . to get in the car and . . . and –

Ollie   And?

Jill   Drive!

Ollie   Drive where?

Jill   *Any*where.

Ollie   In your nightdress?

Jill   I don't care – What's that?

Ollie   My phone.

Jill   You've got a *signal* now?!

Ollie   Text. Unknown sender.

Reads text.

'Enjoy your dream home. Love. Miss Dee.'

Pause.

Ollie   Okay, everyone. It's later now.

Jill   Seven hours later.

Ollie   The sun's coming up.

Jill   We're in the front reception room.

Ollie   We've been talking all night.

Jill   It'd take too long to tell you *everything* we talked about.

Ollie   Most of the time we just went round in circles.

Jill   It'll drive you mad.

Ollie It certainly did me.

Jill We *had* to discuss those things, Ollie.

Ollie I know, I know. But – now! – for everyone's collective sanity we'll condense it all a bit – Ready, sweetheart?

Jill Ready.

Ollie What would you prefer, Jill? Eh? A *new* kitchen? Or a dead body in the *old* one?

Jill Those are my choices?!

Ollie Because – listen, listen! – if it *is* the old one with a corpse I sincerely hope you're ready to face the consequences. Namely, my arrest, a court case and our child growing up with a convicted murderer as a father.

Jill It would be self-defence.

Ollie You never know where the law's concerned.

Jill So you go to jail. At least . . .

Ollie 'At least' *what*, for fuck's sake?

Jill I would've *understood* that. But this . . .

Slight pause.

Ollie When I was at school my best friend was Jeevan. He was the only kid bullied as much as me. One summer two of his cousins were killed in a car crash. When Jeevan told me about it he was so calm. Smiling. I asked him, 'How come you're so happy?' He told me he'd just had a phone call from one of his aunties. Two birds had appeared in her garden. And his auntie – she knew – knew without any doubt whatsoever! – that the two birds were his dead cousins.

Jill . . . What're you saying, Ollie? You killed a vagrant and he's been reincarnated as a designer kitchen?

Ollie   Well . . . yes. Because isn't that quite clearly what *has* happened?

Jill   Well, if it is I want to know *how*! I want to know *why*!

Ollie   I can't tell you that. Any more than Jeevan could give you the how and why about his cousins. He just . . . accepted it.

Jill   And you can do that, can you? Just accept.

Ollie   . . . Why not?

Slight pause.

He starts leaving.

Jill   Wh-where you going?

Ollie   To work on the re-wiring

Jill   *Now*?!

Ollie   I thought you were desperate for a bath.

Jill   Not in *this* house, I'm not. I can't stay here. I *won't*!

He has gone.

Jill   Well, would any of you? Eh? Knowing what's happened? Course not. Nor could any sane person – no, not 'sane'. Anyone with a conscience. Morals. A man died here last night. Oh, I know what some of you are thinking. He was just a vagrant. Why worry? Well, I'm sorry, but I refuse to think like that. 'Love thy neighbour as yourself.' Heard of that? Christian values. It's what I practise. When I see a homeless person on the street I *always* give some money – Oh, don't give me that look. Yes, *you*. I know what you're thinking. 'They'll just spend it on drugs.' Well, *some* might, yes. But surely most just want a sandwich or something – And I know what you're thinking too. 'A bar of soap might do them more good.' And I agree. 'Cleanliness is next to godliness.' But it's not their fault they stink. They've hit hard times – What's that? 'The homeless just lay back and expect us – us! – to take care of them.' Well, yes, again, *some* of them do, I suppose. And – don't get me wrong – I have got no patience with that attitude. How's the old saying go? 'God helps those who help themselves.' Not 'Be as lazy as you like and send the bill to everyone else'. Send it to people like you and me. Right? Oh, yes. Most of them'd suck us dry if they had the chance. I'm well aware of that. My mum worked her fingers – her *arthritic* fingers – to the bone serving them soup and did they ever buy her a little gift as a thank you? No. Not once. Another thing – when you walk past one of them on the street and you don't give any money they mumble something like 'Have a nice day'. You noticed that? Like they're trying to make us feel guilty. Guilty for what? Having self-respect? Aspiring to a better life. Why should I – why should *any* of us? – feel guilty about that? Without us everything out there would fall to pieces. It'd be the Dark Ages all over again. It's people like *us* who're standing between civilisation and chaos – Fuck it, I'm going to the kitchen!

Steps into –

Oh! . . . Oh! . . . Oh! . . . You notice the way the marble shines? . . . Beautiful taps – Hot water! . . . And the cupboards – They're all full of food. *Posh* food! The fridge is full too!

Ollie (*calling, off*)   Jill?

Jill   I'm in here.

He appears.

Jill   Would you like a sandwich or something?

Ollie   Oh . . . Yes. Thank you.

Jill   Salmon and cream cheese?

Ollie   Perfect.

Jill   Drink?

Ollie   Er . . . a juice, I think.

Jill   Orange or – what's this? Elderflower and lime.

Ollie   I'll try that.

Jill   Me too – That's odd.

Ollie   What?

Jill   There's a packet of salmon in the fridge.

Ollie   So?

Jill   So . . . there was only one. And I've just used it.

Ollie   You sure?

Jill   Positive.

Ollie   Take it out.

Jill   What?

Ollie   The salmon in the fridge. Take it out.

Jill   Okay, okay, but what – ?

Ollie   Give it to me – Now, close the fridge door.

Jill   That salmon'll go off if you open it.

Ollie   Look in the fridge again.

Jill   What do'you – ?

Ollie   Just look!

Jill   Oh!

Ollie   More salmon?

Jill   More salmon!

Ollie   Jill! D'you know what this means?!

Jill and **Ollie**   We've got a self-replenishing fridge!

Ollie   No questions. Just accept.

Jill Yum, yum! Lovely sandwich – Oh, don't wash your hands in the kitchen sink, Ollie!

Ollie No hot upstairs. And there won't be. Not if it's left up to me.

Jill But you promised –

Ollie It's too big a job, sweetheart. We'll have to get someone in.

Jill But . . . won't that be . . . difficult now.

Ollie We'll take out a loan.

Jill I'm not talking financially.

Ollie Then what's the – ? . . . Oh!

Jill Exactly. Everything works fine in the kitchen but –

Ollie Nowhere else.

Jill Explain *that*.

Ollie Mmm . . . conundrum.

Slight pause.

Jill Perhaps . . . we don't *have* to explain.

Ollie Oh?

Jill Perhaps we can get – not *just* hot water – but a whole new bathroom. A bathroom every bit as good as this new kitchen.

Ollie . . . Oh, no, Jill. *No.*

Jill What if someone breaks in again.

Ollie I can't believe you're saying this.

Jill Why not?

Ollie *'Why not!'*? . . . It's taking the life of a –

Jill Didn't seem to bother you last night.

Ollie   That's not true. And not fair. What happened last night – it was an accident. What you're asking me to do now –and it is *me* who'll have to do it! Right? – This is premeditated, cold-blooded –

Jill   I want a bloody bath!

Ollie   And you're prepared to *murder* for it?!

Slight pause.

And what if it doesn't work? You thought of that? There's a dead body in the bathroom and it *stays* a dead body.

Jill   I think we should at least . . . try.

Ollie   *Try*?!

Jill   Ollie! It may have slipped your attention but I happen to be pregnant. Do you know what that means? It means I need hygiene. Not for my own personal gratification but for the sake of our baby. Do you want our child to get an infection? *Do* you? Do you want it to be born with brain damage? Deformed? *Both*?!

Slight pause.

Ollie   . . . It's that night.

Jill   We're in the bedroom.

Ollie   I'm holding a knife.

Jill   Shhh!

Ollie   What?

Jill   I thought I heard – Listen!

Ollie   . . . It's nothing.

Jill   Is the back door open?

Ollie   Yes, yes.

Jill   And there's food on the table?

Ollie   You saw me put it there.

Jill   Well, what's bloody wrong with them? Are they all anorexic or something? When I think of how hard we worked to put on that spread. It's sheer ingratitude – Where you going?

Ollie   I'm not doing it.

Jill   But . . . but we *agreed* to –

Ollie   Look at us! Hiding up here like a pair of assassins waiting for someone to – Jesus! What were we thinking? It's madness. No! A sin. I don't believe in heaven and hell, Jill, but I tell you what we've been contemplating doing tonight has taken us further from one and closer to the other.

Jill   Don't say that!

Ollie   I can smell the brimstone. Can't you? Eh?

Jill *doesn't answer.*

Ollie   Now, I am going downstairs and I am going to lock the back door. Then I am going to put this knife back where it belongs. In the knife rack. Then I am going to come back here and we are going to have a good night's sleep like any other normal couple. And in the morning I will arrange for someone to re-wire the house so you can have your bloody bath and –

Jill   How we going to *explain* – ?

Ollie   We'll think of something!

Pause.

I'm opening the bedroom door now . . . walking down the stairs and – What's that? Something's moving in the living room. A man. He's coming towards me. He's wearing a baseball cap. He's eating a Harrods chocolate-covered waffle. He must think the food in the kitchen was a gift. He must think I've come down to welcome him. He smiles. Do I smile back? I think I do. He reaches out to shake my hand. He's very close now. I can smell him. And then . . . it just happened. My arm jolts forward. Stab!

Jill   I hear a noise. I rush out of the bedroom.

Ollie   I'm struggling with the intruder – Stab!

Jill   I see the intruder. He falls to the floor.

Ollie   Then I see –

Jill   There's another intruder!

Ollie   He's coming out of the kitchen.

Jill   He's got a limp.

Ollie   The One with the Baseball Cap looks dead.

Jill   The One with the Limp rushes up to The One with the Baseball Cap.

Ollie   The One with the Limp sees the blood.

Jill   He panics.

Ollie   He pushes past me.

Jill   He opens the front door.

Ollie   He rushes outside –

Jill   KILL HIM!

Ollie   I rush after him. He falls over. I jump on his back. He struggles. Glass and rubble cut his face. I stab him. I feel the blade graze against the bone of his spine. His nylon jacket is gleaming with blood. I stab again. I stab again. I know the exact moment he dies. I feel his life dissolving away. I crawl away from him. Glass and rubble cut my hands.

Slight pause.

Jill   Light! The One with the Baseball Cap – the one still in the hallway – he's starting to sparkle. It's like a million fairy lights twinkling all over him. The fairy lights get bigger. Brighter. They float up. They fill the corridor and stairway. Dazzling. I close my eyes and clutch the banister. I feel the banister change beneath my grip. I feel the staircase change.

And then – the fairy lights fade. I open my eyes. It's the staircase I saw in *Ideal Home Magazine*. The hallway too! Polished floorboards. Walls painted white with a hint of green. Wall lights in the shape of sea shells. Then – More fairy lights! They're coming from outside! It's The One with the Limp. Again I have to close my eyes. The light fades. I open my eyes. I go outside and – A green lawn. Pebble path. And – Oh! Look, Ollie! Look!

Ollie   Leave me alone!

Jill   But the car! The *car*!

He looks.

He gets to his feet.

Ollie   . . . It's the new Lamborghini Huracán LP 610-2 Super Trofeo.

Jill   It's a lovely colour.

Ollie   Nought to seventy in two seconds – oh!

Jill   What?

Ollie   Pocket – Car keys!

Jill   Let's go for a spin.

Ollie   Whoa, whoa! Jesus, Jill. What're you thinking? I kill two people! I stab them to death. Brutally. And then a new car comes along and – shazam! – you think I can just forget all about it?! Just like that? *Eh*?

Jill *and* **Ollie**   YESSSS!

Ollie   Down the motorway!

Jill   It's so smooth!

Ollie   Open a window.

Jill   What do I – ?

Ollie   The button there.

Jill   Wind in my hair.

Ollie   Turn the radio on.

Jill   It's so loud.

Ollie   Subwoofer bass – Change channel.

Jill   What – ?

Ollie   There!

Jill   Oh, I *love* this song.

Ollie   Me too!

Jill and **Ollie** (*singing, heavy-metal style*)
  Make it bigger
  make it brighter
  make it faster
  make it louder
  make it stand out in the crowdier
  for the world to adore
  and when you've done all that –
  oh, hell, I'll still want more.
  Hell, I still want more.

Jill   What you doing?

Ollie   Parking.

Jill   Here? Why?

Ollie   The view!

Jill   View?! It's the middle of the night!?

Ollie   That's why it's special – Come on!

Jill   I am not climbing that hill.

He picks her up.

Jill   Ooo – ha, ha! Why, Mister Swift, what big muscles you have – Careful! Baby!

Ollie   You're both safe with me.

Jill   Yes . . . yes, we are.

He carries her up hill.

Ollie   . . . Well?

Jill   Oh! Oh, Ollie!

Ollie   I told you.

They gaze at the view . . .

Jill   . . . Everywhere is orange and gleaming . . . fiery. Burning. Like we're on top of a volcano or something. The lights of the cars on the motorway . . . a river of lava. And the sky . . . red . . . Clouds of smouldering ash. I wouldn't be surprised if some fire-breathing monster came swooping down all fangs and claws. I never thought something like this could be beautiful.

Ollie   But it is.

Jill   . . . It is.

Slight pause.

Ollie   If we're going to carry on . . .

Jill   The renovations?

Ollie   Yes.

Jill   Oh, I think we should.

Ollie   So do I. But . . .

Jill   Mmm?

Ollie   We can't have any more . . . messiness.

Jill   Not like tonight.

Ollie   No – Not for *my* sake, you understand.

Jill   Of course not. For *their* sake.

Ollie   Exactly.

Jill   The renovations have to be . . .

Ollie   Stress free.

Jill   Humane.

Ollie   Quick.

Jill   . . . Any ideas?

Ollie   . . . Not yet. But I'll think of something.

Jill   You're so clever – And, Ollie?

Ollie   Yes, sweetheart?

Jill   I can't see *any* of it. It'll upset baby.

Ollie   Of course. *I'll* do it all.

Jill   And I don't want to know . . . anything about them.

Ollie   Of course.

Jill   Don't *ever* tell me their names.

Ollie   Never.

Jill   And we can't wait for them to break in.

Ollie   No, no, of course.

Jill   Nothing's guaranteed.

Ollie   We're not in control.

Jill   Exactly. You'll have to get in the car and . . .

Ollie   Find them.

Jill   Oh, sweetheart.

Ollie   Sweetheart.

They go to kiss but –

Jill   . . . The ones you choose . . .

Ollie   Go on.

Jill They should only be the ones who . . . *deserve* it.

Ollie *Deserve* it?

Jill The ones who will never . . . contribute.

Ollie Of course . . . The scum.

Jill The scroungers.

Ollie The spongers.

Jill The vermin – Aw!

Ollie What?

Jill Baby.

Ollie He moved?!

Jill Feel!

He touches her belly.

Ollie There! Ha! He's saying, 'Let me out of here!'

Jill We've got your dream home to get ready first.

Slight pause.

Ollie Next day. I've been trying to solve the problem of humane home renovation. As you can see, the floor's covered with all sorts of stuff and . . . well, after many hours of trial and error – mainly error, I admit – I've finally come up with something that I think – I *hope* – ticks all the boxes. Okay. So . . . Most important thing – speed! Right? It has to be quick! Now, I can guess what you're thinking. Gun. And, yes, that was my first thought too. But there's problems. One, I've never shot a gun before. Okay, okay, I can get one and practise. Fair enough. But that still leaves problem two – noise. Guns go bang. Okay, I can get a silencer. But that still leaves – three! What if the first bullet don't do the trick? Even a bullet in the head's not always fatal. And, believe me, I do not want to be pumping bullet after bullet into some writhing mass at my feet. Well, would you? Be honest. No.

Not fair on me, not fair on them. What's the alternative?
Strangulation? Takes too long. And all that protruding
tongue and bulging eyes stuff? No thank you. Gassing? Too
complicated to set up. So that leaves . . . Electricity! Yesss!
Fast. Silent. Clean. And so – da-dahh! This is the magic wand
I made for Dad's act. Sparks used to shoot out the end –
here. But now – as you can see – I've adapted it somewhat so
that –

Jill   Coffee?

Ollie   Thanks.

Jill   Oh, what a mess.

Ollie   Don't touch anything!

Jill   What're you doing with that old thing?

Ollie   *This* is the answer to our prayers. Think cattle prod
times a million. Simply plug it into any normal household
socket. And before you say –

Jill and **Ollie**   None of the sockets work.

Ollie   They *do* in the kitchen. And before you say –

Jill and **Ollie**   It's the *bathroom* we want renovated.

Ollie   I've got an extension that'll reach the bathroom.

Jill   I have married a genius.

Ollie   Hang on, hang on. There's something else I need to
say. *Suggest.*

Jill   What's that?

Ollie   You're not going to like it.

Jill   Go on.

Ollie   We should renovate the garage first.

Jill   The garage?!

Ollie   We can't leave a car like that on the street, Jill.

Jill   I am *not* going another night without a bath!

Ollie   The car attracts too much attention.

Jill   No! We've *got* to have a bathroom! – You all agree with me, don't you?

Ollie   Don't drag *them* into it!

Jill   Why not? – A bathroom! Right? *She* agrees with me. You see? And *she's* nodding too.

Ollie   *He's* not. Nor is he.

Jill   We'll have a vote.

Ollie   A *what*? – Oh, no, Jill. Jesus.

Jill   Everyone. What's more important, a garage to stop a car getting wet in the rain –

Ollie (*overlapping*)   It's not to stop it getting wet in the rain.

Jill (*overlapping*)   – or a functioning bathroom in a family home especially when one of the inhabitants is heavily pregnant and in need of constant hygiene to prevent her child being born with physical deformity –

Ollie (*overlapping*)   This isn't fair! It's not!

Jill (*overlapping*)   – or brain damage or, more than likely, both. Show of hands please. Ready? Who thinks bathroom? Show of hands for hygienic bathroom. Think of the baby . . . Thank you. Now . . . garage? . . . I win.

Ollie   Are you sure?

Jill   Yes. Night-time. You're out in the car searching for renovators. Go on.

Ollie   Everyone, we'll just skip the details of this next bit because – in short – it was a total washout.

Jill   No one would get in the car.

Ollie   They were suspicious.

Jill   Of *him*?!

Ollie   Of *me*?! So. The next day –

Jill   I'm in the bedroom.

Ollie   I'm outside washing the car.

Walks off.

Jill   I'm trying to solve the problem of Suspicion Free
Renovator Collection. Now, I've had an idea that might work
. . . but it means sorting through some boxes of old clothes
because I need . . . to find – Aha! Ollie's old polo neck.
That's what I'm after – Hang on! Can you hear voices? . . .
Ollie's talking to someone.

Goes to window.

Who's that? He's very smart. He's getting in his car. He's
driving away.

Ollie *walks on.*

Ollie   That was Rashid.

Jill   *Who?*

He hands her a business card.

Jill (*reading*)   'Rashid Webb. Viva Sunshine Property'.

Ollie   They represent all the other houses on the Close.
And the streets around. He said they'd all but written off the
whole area. He loved what we're doing to the house. Took
photos. Said it'll help sell the other houses.

Jill   That's wonderful news.

Ollie   Yeah, but you know what it means, Jill.

Jill   It means Miss Dee was right.

Ollie   It means *neighbours* . . . *Watching*.

Jill   . . . Oh.

Ollie   Oh.

Jill   Well . . . no one'll know what we get up to *inside* the house.

Ollie   And outside? The garage? Garden?

Jill   We'll just have to do those renovations quickly.

Ollie   Quickly's not likely if last night's anything to go by.

Jill   Aha! I've been thinking about that and – Voila!

Ollie   What's that?

Jill   Your white polo neck.

Ollie   Jesus. Thought we'd chucked that out.

Jill   Glad we didn't because – with this . . .

Ollie   Oh, that never suited me.

Jill   But – look, look! – if you wear the polo neck . . . under the black jacket . . . like this – See?

Ollie   . . . What?

Jill   The white bit showing at the collar.

Ollie   . . . I am *not* impersonating a priest, Jill!

Jill   You won't be *impersonating* anyone. If other people happen to *mistake* you for one, that's *their* problem. And here – I found some old flyers Mum made when she ran the church hostel. It mentions hot food and a bath. Here's a crucifix.

Ollie   Jill, Jill . . . I'll be a priest in a state-of-the-art Lamborghini.

Jill   A *Catholic* priest. No problem.

Ollie   It won't work.

Jill   It will.

Ollie   It won't.

Jill   It will.

Ollie   It did. I see someone huddled by a cash machine. He's got a blanket round his shoulders. I park the car nearby. 'Hello, my son. Please allow me to help you.' I hand him one of the flyers. 'I can offer you a hot meal and a place to sleep.' He gives a whistle as he approaches the car. I tell him it was a gift from the Pope for all the work I did with the lepers of Mozambique. I open a window to let out the stink of him. I drive back to the house as fast as I can. He wipes his feet on the doormat. 'Would you like a hot bath, my son?' We go upstairs. I open the bathroom door. He steps inside.

Jill   I'm waiting in the kitchen downstairs.

Ollie   I pick up the wand and touch it to the back of his head –

Jill and **Ollie**   BZZZZZ!

Ollie   . . . *JILL*!

She rushes to him.

Jill   It's the bathroom I saw in *Best Bathroom Magazine*.

Ollie   After that the renovations – oh, they happened quickly.

Jill   One a night.

Ollie   Garage.

Jill   Back garden.

Ollie   Our bedroom.

Jill   Utility room.

Ollie   Spare bedroom.

Jill   Lounge.

Ollie   Downstairs hallway.

Jill   Upstairs hallway.

Ollie Loft.

Jill It all looked wonderful!

Ollie There's only one room we couldn't get right.

Jill and **Ollie** The nursery.

Ollie We tried five nights on the trot.

Jill Six.

Ollie Jill, Jill, I've just realised. We need to . . . to *clarify* . . .

Jill 'Clarify'?

Ollie This . . . doing the same room over and over.

Jill Of course! Sorry, everyone. Here we are gabbling on –

Ollie And we haven't told you about –

Jill Things we discovered –

Ollie The Rules of Renovation – Shall I – ?

Jill Yes, yes, go ahead.

Ollie Okay. So. What did we learn from the initial renovation? Renovator ceases to function in the kitchen. Result? Kitchen undergoes a renovation. Conclusion? Renovation occurs in the room – or area – where renovator ceases to function. But there was something about this that . . . well it just niggled me.

Jill The time gap.

Ollie Between the magic-wanding –

Jill And the fairy lights.

Ollie Sixty-six point six seconds.

Jill So he decided to carry out an experiment.

Ollie I used the wand in the bathroom.

Jill Then quickly dragged the renovator to the hallway.

Ollie   Fairy lights in hallway. Result?

Jill   Hallway renovated

Ollie   Conclusion?

Jill   It's not where the *magic-wanding* happens.

Ollie   It's where the *fairy lights* happen.

Jill   This is important because –

Ollie   The wand can be used at the front door –

Jill and **Ollie**   BZZZZZ!

Ollie   Then the renovator dragged to any part of the house –

Jill   Anywhere a renovation's needed.

Ollie   And that leads on to –

Jill   The other thing we discovered.

Ollie   Purely by accident.

Ollie   It was the night we intended to do . . . what was it?

Jill   The cellar. He used the wand at the front door.

Ollie   I start to drag the renovator – Aww!

Jill   His back.

Ollie   I couldn't move!

Jill   Fairy lights in hallway!

Ollie   Result?

Jill   Hallway renovated!

Ollie   For the *second* time.

Jill   With the full-length mirror I wanted.

Ollie   Conclusion?

Jill   Things can be renovated more than once.

Ollie   Hence the umpteen attempts at the nursery.

Jill   Neighbours!

Ollie   Eh? What?

Jill   We got our first neighbours.

Ollie   Oh! Right. Yes.

Jill   They moved into number one.

Ollie   A couple.

Jill   A bit younger than us.

Ollie   Mitch.

Jill   And Brandy.

Ollie   Models.

Jill   Not catwalk stuff.

Ollie   Catalogues.

Jill   Selling things.

Ollie   We showed them round the house.

Jill   They *loved* it.

Ollie   *Loved* it. Only one problem.

Jill   They knew the price of *everything*.

Ollie   'That Moroccan-style water feature costs a fortune – Don't it, Brand.'

Jill   'The plumbing alone could break the bank.'

Ollie   Jill panicked.

Jill   I did.

Ollie   What did you say?

Jill   Oh, Ollie did all that. He's Mr DIY.

Ollie   Big mistake.

Jill   Huge.

Ollie   Because –

Jill   Any problem Mitch and Brandy had –

Ollie   They asked *me* to help.

Jill   He practically fitted their bathroom!

Ollie   I *did* fit their bathroom.

Jill   But . . . while all that was a bit of a pain –

Ollie   Which it was.

Jill   It was *still* good to have neighbours.

Ollie   It was.

Jill   You should hear him and Mitch talk about cars.

Ollie   What about you and Brandy?

Jill   Brandy was trying for a baby.

Ollie   She brought over piles of catalogues.

Jill   Good thing she did because – Look at this, Ollie!

Ollie   What's that?

Jill   I've found it! The perfect nursery.

Ollie   If that's what you *want*, then that's what you'll *get*.

Jill   Go on, then.

Ollie   What?

Jill   Get a renovator.

Ollie   But . . . there's snooker on the telly and –

Jill   You'd rather watch snooker than give our child –

Ollie   I've been out every night since we moved here, Jill.

Jill   Oh, you do exaggerate.

Ollie   I am *not* exager –

Jill   Look. Once baby's born there won't be any more renovations. There can't be. Not with a child in the house. You can flop in front of the telly and watch as much snooker as you like.

Ollie   Promise?

Jill   Promise – Are you in the car?

Ollie   I am! I spy a possible renovator –

Jill   Bring it back!

Ollie   'This is where I live, my child . . . It is a nice front garden, isn't it – Oh, hello, Mitch! – It's just my neighbour coming over, my child, don't worry. Just get inside the house. Stay in the hallway. That's it. Thank you, my child – Mitch! What can I do for you, mate? . . . Yes, it is late and I'm just . . . just helping someone – What? . . . A leak? Well, have you tried turning the water off? . . . Okay, okay. Go back! I'll be right over . . . Sorry about that, my child. I'm afraid one of my parishioners needs help with a little plumbing problem. Can I ask you to wait in the back garden till I return . . . That's it . . . Outside . . . Thank you . . .

Jill   What's going on?

Ollie   Mitch. Water leak.

Jill   *Now*?

Ollie   I won't be long.

Jill   But where's the – ?

Ollie   Garden.

Jill   Oh, Ollie.

Ollie   Don't worry. You won't see them.

Jill   I can *smell* them.

Ollie   Go back upstairs.

Rushes out.

She just about to go back upstairs when –

Kay   Hello.

Miss Dee *has appeared as* **Kay**.

Jill   Oh . . . you're . . .

Kay   The thing you can smell, yeah.

Jill   Oh, I . . . I didn't mean to –

Kay   What's your name?

Jill   . . . Jillian.

Kay   Is the baby you're expecting Father Oliver's?

Jill   'Father –'? . . . Oh . . . yes. It is.

Kay   I don't judge. The celibacy rules are bonkers anyway. We all need a kiss and a cuddle – When's it due?

Jill   . . . Sixteen weeks.

Kay   Boy or girl?

Jill   Boy.

Kay   Have you thought of a name?

Jill   Benjamin.

Kay   Is that a saint or something?

Jill   No, it's . . . it was my dad's name.

Kay   Please don't be scared of me.

Jill   I . . . I'm not.

Kay   You are. I'm not crazy. Can I have something to drink please?

Jill   Oh . . . Yes, of course. Juice?

Kay   Why not.

Jill   Pomegranate?

Kay   I've never had that.

Jill *goes to get juice.*

Kay   Is this you in the white dress?

Jill   What's that?

Kay   The photo on the wall.

Jill   Oh. Yes. My confirmation.

Kay   Confirma – ? Oh. Religion.

Jill *returns with drink.*

Jill   After Dad died . . . my mum . . . well, she –

Kay   Faith can be a great comfort.

Jill   . . . It can be.

Gives **Kay** *drink.*

Kay   Thank you.

Drinks.

Oh . . . it's very nice. Very refreshing and . . . clean . . .

Starts to cry.

Jill   Oh, don't.

Kay   I'm sorry.

Jill   Please. Here – sit down.

Kay   I'll make your sofa dirty.

Jill   It doesn't matter.

Kay   It does. I'll sit on the floor.

Jill   Oh, you can't –

Kay   *Please*, Jill. I'd prefer it.

Kay *sits on floor.*

Slight pause.

Jill   What's your name?

Kay   Kay.

Jill   Where's your family, Kay?

Kay   Miles away.

Jill   Did you . . .? I mean, how long have you –?

Kay   I ran away when I was fifteen.

Jill   Can I ask . . .? No, it's none of my business.

Kay   I've got a brother. His name's Barney. He's five years younger than me. He could spin a football on the tip of his finger. When he was nine he got ill. Acute lymphatic leukaemia. The house stank of medicine. I met a boy I liked once. It was all going fine till he found out about Barney. 'I wanna have fun not worry about your brother dropping dead all the time.'

Jill   That's a *terrible* thing to say.

Kay   I still loved Barney. But sometimes . . . Oh, he was a bossy little bastard. Me and Barney were alone in the house one day. I was in the kitchen trying to do some revision. I could hear Barney in the living room playing a computer game. Then the game stopped. It all goes quiet. I call out, 'You okay?' He calls back, 'Yeah'. That's what it's like. When you're looking after someone. There's no relaxing. Not for a second. You have a knot in your belly. It never goes away. You won't understand.

Jill   I do a bit. My mum had arthritis.

Kay   Did it turn *her* into a bossy bastard too?

Jill   Sometimes.

Kay   Did you feel like hitting her?

Jill   Well . . . I don't think I –

Kay   I hit Barney. The day he dropped his mobile phone. He called out for me to pick it up. I pick it up. I go back to revising. He calls again. 'I'm hungry.' I make him a sandwich. 'Not enough butter!' I get more butter. 'I want the crusts cut off!' I cut the crusts off. 'I need to go to the toilet.' I'm helping him walk to the toilet. 'Ahhh! That hurts! You know it hurts if you touch me there! You're useless!' And suddenly I'm hitting him. Punches! He falls over. I'm get on top of him. I hit him and hit him. 'Why don't you just die! *Die*!'

Slight pause.

I'm in my bedroom when Mum and Dad get back. I hear Barney telling them what's happened. I wait for Dad's footsteps up the stairs. But . . . no one came. An hour goes by. Two. Then a gentle rap on the door. It's Mum. She's brought me a cup of tea. She's all smiles. It's as if nothing has happened.

Jill   She's forgiven you.

Kay   I don't *want* to be forgiven. I want to be kicked from one side of the room to the other.

Slight pause.

The next day I get up and have breakfast. I put my school books in my satchel. I kiss Mum goodbye and walk out of the house. I walk down the main road, past the school, down to the next main road, round the roundabout, down the motorway, I just keep walking and walking.

Jill   And you never go back?

Kay   . . . No.

Jill   Have you . . . phoned?

Kay   No.

Jill   So your brother . . .?

Kay   He's probably dead.

Slight pause.

Jill *holds* **Kay**'s *hand.*

Jill   You must be hungry.

Kay   I am.

Jill   How does a salmon and cranberry baguette sound?

Kay   Like something from a restaurant.

Jill   Why don't you watch television – Here!

Turns the telly on.

Kay   The screen's huge!

Jill   What d'you want to watch?

Kay   Something silly.

Jill   Cartoons?

Kay   Yes!

Jill   . . . There we go! Now, let's get you that sandwich.

Leaves.

Kay *settles to watch television.*

Ollie *enters.*

Ollie   You've made yourself comfortable.

Kay   Oh, hello, Father. Jill said it was okay.

Ollie   You've *spoken* to her?!

Kay   She's in the kitchen.

Ollie   Now, everyone, I thought I should explain what's going on in my head right now. So. Renovator – there! Jill – kitchen! My assessment of what's happened – Jill and renovator met somehow. Jill panicked and plonked renovator in front of television while she went to hide in the kitchen. Conclusion – Jill is too close for me to use wand down here. I will pick wand up – which I am now doing – and persuade renovator to – Would you like to have a quick bath, my child?

Kay   I'll have my sandwich first if that's okay.

Ollie   But . . . wouldn't you like to be *clean* first?

Kay   I'm very hungry.

Ollie   *God* would like you to be clean.

Kay   Oh . . . okay.

Starts to follow **Ollie** *as –*

Jill *enters from kitchen and –*

Jill   Ollie! No!

Ollie   Go back to the kitchen, Jill.

Jill   I've made Kay a sandwich.

Ollie   You know her name?!

Kay   What's that you're holding, Father?

Ollie   It's a . . . a . . .

Kay   It looks like a magic wand – Jill?

Jill   Yes, it . . . it is a sort of magic wand.

Kay   What does it do?

Slight pause.

. . . Are you going to kill me?

Slight pause.

Jill. I like you. You too, Father. I know you're both good people. I have an *instinct* for these things. I'm not going to run. I don't *want* to run. I just . . . I just want to know what's going on.

Slight pause.

Jill   . . . Ollie's not a priest –

Ollie   Jill!

Jill   She deserves to know the truth! . . . Ollie and me –
we're married and . . . when we first moved into this house –
it was a wreck. And then, one night, there was . . . a break-in.
Ollie struggled with the intruder and he . . . he –

Kay   I know what you're going to say.

Jill   Oh, no, Kay, you . . . you can't.

Kay   There's rumours. On the street. Stories whispered
round the campfires at night. I heard them first in another
city. Miles from here. The rumours say they're people who
drive round in their cars at night. They pick up the homeless
– like me – and take us home. They kill us. And as we die our
bodies glow. Glows so bright it's like we've swallowed
sunshine. When the glow has faded away . . . our bodies
have gone. But the room all round – it has been
transformed. New furniture. New wallpaper. New . . .
whatever the killers wish for. The rumours say the
government's in on it. And the police.

Slight pause.

I should be scared. But I'm not. Just the opposite. I feel . . .
calm. More calm than I've felt in a long time. It's as if . . . all
my stumbling, all my mistakes, everything has led me here.
For the first time in my life, I'm exactly where I should be.

Jill   But Kay –

Kay   I want to be part of your home, Jill, Father – Oh, yes,
yes, I know you're not really a priest. But in my eyes . . . you
are. Only a man of God could've offered me . . . this chance
– That thing you're holding. Is that what will . . .?

Ollie   Yes.

Kay   Will it . . . hurt?

Jill   Oh, no. No.

Kay   . . . What room do you want me to . . .?

Jill   The nursery.

Kay   Oh! Bless you. To feel such . . . purpose . . . such meaning – Tears! You see? It's upstairs, I take it.

Ollie   . . . Yes.

Kay   Lead the way, Father – Are coming with us, Jillian?

Jill   I'd . . . I'd rather not. Do you mind?

Kay   Of course not. Can I give you a kiss?

Jill *nods.*

Kay *kisses* **Jill***.*

Kay   Tell Benjamin about me. Tell him you once met someone . . . and they weren't as scary as they looked.

Ollie *and* **Kay** *go upstairs.*

Slight pause.

Ollie *and* **Jill**   BZZZZZ!

Jill *clutches belly.*

Jill   Ollie! . . . *OLLIE*!

Ollie *rushes on and* –

Ollie   Now?!

Jill   NOW!

Ollie *and* **Jill** (*singing brightly, from Handel's* Messiah)
    For unto us a child is born
    Until us a son is given
    And the government shall be
    upon his shoulders –

Jill   Well, here he is, everyone!

Ollie   Baby Benjamin!

Jill   When I first put him in my arms –

Ollie   Oh, my God!

Jill   It was like –

Ollie   Amazing!

Jill   Like I'd been . . . been plugged into everything.

Ollie   His little hand grabbing my finger . . . and . . .

Jill   Oh, don't upset yourself sweetheart.

Ollie   Benjy – he was in an incubator.

Jill   I had the infection from hell.

Ollie   I kept thinking . . . if anything happened to either of you . . .

Jill   It's alright, sweetheart, it's alright.

Ollie   I'd kill myself. I would.

Jill   Nothing's going to happen to us. Come on. We're in the car.

Ollie   'In the – ?'

Jill   I've just been discharged from hospital. You're driving us home. Ready?

Ollie   . . . Ready. You . . . you see the streets, sweetheart?

Jill   More and more people are moving in.

Ollie   There's even scaffolding going up the car plant.

Jill   What're they turning that into I wonder?

Ollie   No idea – Oh! There's something I haven't told you.

Jill   What's that?

Ollie   We've got new neighbours. House number four.

Jill   When did *they* move in?

Ollie   Day after you went into hospital.

Jill   That was nearly three weeks ago!

Ollie   I've had a few things on my mind, Jill.

Jill   Okay, okay. What're they like?

Ollie   Very friendly. Nishaka and Aashiyana. Doctors. They've got an eight-year-old son. Navneet. And listen to this . . . Guess what they paid for their house.

Jill   Tell me.

Ollie   *Twice* what Brandy and Mitch paid for theirs.

Jill   *No*?!

Ollie   We're in a property hot spot.

Jill   And it's *our* house that got it started.

Ollie   Talking of which –

Jill   We're home, Benjy!

Ollie   Benjy likes his cot.

Jill   Oh . . . look at him, Ollie. Look.

Ollie   We've got everything we could ever want.

Jill   We have . . . Almost.

Ollie   *Almost*? . . . Whoa, whoa! You don't mean –

Jill   Let me explain.

Ollie   You *promised*, Jill. Once Benjy's is born. No more renovations.

Jill   It's *because* Benjy's here there *has* to be more.

Ollie   I don't see how –

Jill   Let me explain.

Ollie   But –

Jill   *Please*, sweetheart . . . While I was in hospital – the other mothers – they all talked about things they wanted for their baby. They showed me catalogues I'd never even heard of.

Ollie   Here we go.

Jill   Wonderful catalogues full of wonderful things – A ceiling made of lights and sounds.

Ollie   Lights and sounds?!

Jill   It's called the Celestial Ceiling Cerebral Enhancer. It improves babies' intelligence. You want Benjy to go to university, don't you?

Ollie   Of course I do but –

Jill   And a wall-to-wall aquarium.

Ollie   In a nursery?!

Jill   Downstairs.

Ollie   I hate aquariums.

Jill   I've seen the perfect cocktail cabinet too.

Ollie   We don't even drink.

Jill   Our *neighbours* will. I want us to have soirées.

Ollie   Soirées?!

Jill   Dinner parties.

Ollie   And all this is for *Benjy*, is it?

Jill   Ollie, we are in a property hot spot. You said that yourself. You know what that means. It means our neighbours will get richer and richer. They'll have better bathrooms than ours. Better kitchens than ours. They'll be able to buy their children everything they want. Do you want Benjamin to grow up feeling like a second-class citizen in his own neighbourhood?

Ollie   Of course I don't.

Jill   I know what's bothering you. You don't want to be out every night. You want to be snuggled up on the sofa watching telly with me and the baby.

Ollie   I do.

Jill   That's what *I* want too. So I've thought of a way to speed things up.

Ollie   'Speed things up'?

Jill   One of the mothers in the maternity ward had her baby in a birthing pool. She asked me and a few others to be there with her. She joked how we could all get in the water. And that's when I had the idea . . . Shall I carry on?

Ollie   Can I stop you?

Jill   *Our* bath – we could get four in there easy. Perhaps five. And the wand – it's electric. So stick it in the water and – BZZZZZ!

Slight pause.

Ollie   . . . One problem.

Jill   I know what you're going to say.

Ollie   I thought you would.

Jill   'If they're all magic-wanded in the same place how am I going to get *five* renovators to different parts of the house in – ?'

Ollie   Sixty-six point six seconds. I'll never do it.

Jill   Not *alone* you won't.

Ollie   Are you . . . are you saying what I think you're –

Jill   I'll help you.

Ollie   But I thought you –

Jill   Baby's changed everything!

Ollie   Jill, dragging a body is not easy.

Jill   It can't be trickier than changing the duvet cover.

Ollie   It can be *heavier*.

Jill   Then you'll just have to make sure some of the renovators are . . . smaller framed.

Ollie   'Smaller framed'? . . . You don't mean . . .?

Jill   What?

Ollie   . . . Children.

Jill   *Children*?! For the love of God, Ollie, of *course* I don't mean children.

Ollie   Sorry, sorry.

Jill   I'm a *mother*!

Ollie   It was a stupid thing to say.

Jill   It reveals more about *you* than it does about *me*.

Ollie   I know. My mind. Ugh! Yours? Yum. Okay?

Jill   . . . Thank you.

Slight pause.

Ollie   *If* we're going to fill the bath with renovators . . .

Jill   Mmm?

Ollie   Then on any one night . . . It'll have to be same-sex renovation.

Jill   Of course. This is a respectable home.

Ollie   So . . . on the nights it *is* only women –

Jill   I'll take them up to the bath.

Ollie   You'll have to get them naked and –

Jill   I *know* what I have to do, Ollie. It's fine.

Ollie Okay.

Jill Okay.

Ollie And . . . I will *not* be out every night?

Jill No.

Ollie I *mean* it, Jill.

Jill I mean it too. You'll just be out . . .

Ollie Mmm?

Jill Once a week?

Ollie Once a month.

Jill Once a fortnight.

Ollie . . . When shall we start?

Jill Oh, there's no rush? . . . Tonight.

Ollie 'Hello, I'm Father Oliver. Let me offer you food and –'

Jill Welcome!

Ollie Sister Jillian! We have three dear friends in need of succour.

Jill Only three?

Ollie Sister Jillian always wants to help as many as possible.

Jill God bless you, few as you are.

Ollie This is Margaret, Iris . . . and this 'smaller framed' bag of skin and bone is Terri.

Jill Perfect – What I mean is . . .

Ollie Perfect to fatten up with lots and lots of food.

Jill Of course. Bless them.

Ollie Bless them.

Jill Bless them. Would you like a bath, my children?

Ollie I bet they would. Would you take them up, Sister?

Jill Of course. Oh, Father! Will you keep an eye on the beef and dumpling casserole I've got in the oven?

Ollie Of course, Sister Jillian.

Jill This way, my children . . . Here's the bathroom. I'll just turn the water on. Take your clothes off. Would you like some bubble bath? We have lavender and jasmine – What's that? Oh, this thing. Yes, it does look like a magic wand, doesn't it.

Ollie and **Jill** BZZZZZ!

Jill Champagne!

Ollie But we don't drink!

Jill One glass! What harm can it do?

Ollie . . . You're right. A toast.

Jill Home sweet home.

Jill and **Ollie** Home sweet home.

Ollie And that's how it went on.

Jill Every fortnight –

Ollie Four or five renovations.

Jill One time – Six.

Ollie Six is our record.

Jill And – to be fair – the night we had six . . . well, it wasn't a total success, was it, sweetheart?

Ollie No, it wasn't.

Jill Shall we tell them.

Ollie Yeah, why not.

Jill   Oh, it's *so* funny everyone.

Ollie   We manage to get five out of the bath –

Jill   But the *sixth* renovator.

Ollie   I couldn't get a grip.

Jill   He was covered with soap.

Ollie   That bloody bubble bath.

Jill   He kept splashing back in the water.

They're both laughing.

Ollie   More bubbles.

Jill   They went in his eyes.

Ollie   I slipped over.

Jill   I rushed to help

Ollie   She slipped over.

Jill   Thump! Right on my backside!

Ollie   The renovator was flopping all over the place.

Jill   It was like something from a silent comedy.

Ollie   Pure slapstick!

Jill   We were still in the bathroom when the fairy lights happened.

Ollie   But Jill – she didn't have any new ideas.

Jill   I didn't!

Ollie   So the bathroom –

Ollie and **Jill**   It stayed the same! – HA, HA, HA!

Their laughter fades.

Ollie   Is that your phone?

Jill   Eh? What?

Ollie   It's the day you get the phone call.

Jill   You mean . . . 'that' phone call.

Ollie   Yes. 'That' phone call.

She is hesitant.

Ollie   It has to come sometime, sweetheart.

Jill   . . . We're snuggled up watching telly.

Ollie   Your phone rings.

Jill   Number's not recognised. Oh, it must be Miss Dee! (*Answers phone.*) Hello, Miss Dee?! . . . Oh. Sorry, I thought you were . . . someone else . . . Of *course* you're not a disappointment . . . Yes, yes, it has been a long time, Father Vianney . . . How did you get my –? . . . Oh, I see . . . I see . . . A boy, that's right . . . Ten months and two weeks . . . Yes, of course . . . Let me speak to Oliver and we'll get back to you . . . Bye, Father. Yes, yes, God bless.

Hangs up.

Ollie   How did he get your new number?

Jill   Someone from the hospital.

Ollie   They had no right to give –

Jill   They probably thought we'd *want* to hear from –

Ollie   Well, we *don't*! – He was asking about the baptism wasn't he.

She doesn't answer.

Ollie   Tell him to stuff it. I went along with the church wedding thing because you wanted it. You and your mum. But I am *not* indoctrinating Benjy to –

Jill   For the sake of his immortal soul, Father Vianney said.

Ollie   Of *course* he'd say that! It's his job. We made a deal on this, Jill!

Jill   Immortal soul! Our child.

Slight pause.

Ollie   I'm having another drink.

Jill   Well then so will I.

Ollie   Don't get drunk on me now.

Jill   I might enjoy it.

Ollie   You won't enjoy the hangover – Shall we have another toast?

Jill   No.

Knocks back her drink.

He drinks his.

Slight pause.

Jill   Okay. What next?

Ollie   . . . New neighbours?

Jill   Miriam and Jonny.

Ollie   They moved into number two.

Jill   In their forties?

Ollie   Oh, Jonny's fifty.

Jill   He used to be a judge.

Ollie   Had a breakdown or something.

Jill   'I blame it on the things he heard in court.'

Ollie   'N-n-no. I loved my j-j-job.'

Ollie   They would be the perfect neighbours –

Jill   Except for one thing –

Ollie   Their children.

Jill   Twins.

Ollie Both fifteen.

Jill Tristan and Tina.

Ollie 'Look at all the stuff you've got.'

Jill 'How can you afford it?'

Ollie 'You must be rich.'

Jill This time . . . I didn't panic.

Ollie Answer prepared.

Jill We inherited some money.

Ollie From my dad.

Jill And from my mum.

Ollie That shut them up.

Jill A few weeks after they moved in –

Ollie They had an antique chair delivered –

Jill Miriam loved antiques.

Ollie She called us over to see it.

Jill 'It's a Louise Quinze chaise longue.'

Ollie 'Isn't it to d-d-die for.'

Jill Die?! . . . *Die*?!

Rushes away.

Ollie Jill? – I'm sorry, Jonny, Miriam . . . Jill! Why rush off like that?

Jill What did he mean?

Ollie Who?

Jill Jonny. 'To d-d-die for.'

Ollie It's just . . . it's just an expression.

She stares.

Ollie   Sweetheart . . . are you alright?

Jill   Why shouldn't I be alright? . . . That's Benjy.

Ollie   I'll go.

Leaves.

She starts to look around at everyone.

She's trying to say something.

The words won't come.

She keeps trying.

Nothing.

Then . . .

She flinches as if she's heard something.

She looks all round.

She flinches again . . . again . . .

She is becoming increasingly fearful.

She starts to let out tiny gasps.

She gets more and more agitated.

Her gasps get louder until –

She screams!

Ollie *rushes back.*

Ollie   Jill! Jesus, what's wrong?

Jill   The olives.

Ollie   Olives?

Jill   Look!

Ollie   I *am* looking and –

Jill   They're eyes. Human eyes.

Ollie Jill . . .

Jill I *saw* them!

Ollie Shush, shush . . . They are *not* eyes, sweetheart. Look – My phone! The whole Close must've heard you. It's Mitch.

Answers phone.

Hey, Mitch! . . . No, no, everything's just fine, mate. Jill had a . . . She thought she saw a mouse. Didn't. Thought she did . . . Ha, ha, yes, mate . . . Ha, ha . . . Thanks for calling. Love to Brandy. Bye, mate.

Hangs up.

They face each other.

Ollie We have to . . . we have to keep calm, Jill.

She doesn't answer.

Ollie *Jill*!

Jill Yes! We do . . . I *am*.

Ollie We love our baby.

Jill We love our baby.

Ollie We'd do anything for him.

Jill We'd do anything for him.

Ollie We're doing nothing wrong.

Jill We're doing nothing wrong.

Ollie Say it again.

Jill We're doing nothing wrong.

Ollie . . . Perhaps . . . an early night?

Jill Yes. I'd *love* an early night.

Ollie I'll make you some hot milk.

Jill Mum swore by hot milk.

Ollie Here it is.

Jill Mmm, delicious.

Ollie You're looking more relaxed already.

Jill I'm feeling more relaxed already.

Ollie Shall I turn the lights out?

Jill Please. Goodnight.

Ollie Goodnight.

Jill Kiss.

Ollie Kiss.

Slight pause.

Next day!

She gasps.

Ollie What *now*?

Jill The sofa!

Ollie 'The – ?'

Jill Feel it.

Ollie I don't –

Jill Just fucking feel it!

Ollie What am I supposed to be –

Jill Human hair!

Ollie *What!?*

Jill There's human hair growing on our sofa.

Ollie No.

Jill Feel it again . . . *Feel* it!

Ollie Two days later – Have you seen this?

Jill   What?

Ollie   In the local newspaper. Some conglomerate has bought the old car plant apparently. They're going to turn it into a shopping centre. The biggest in the country. A spokesperson said, 'This up-and-coming area is the perfect spot for The Never Enough shopping experience.' That's what they're calling it. The Never Enough Shopping Centre. Because – and I quote – 'Enough is never enough.' . . . Are you listening, Jill?

Slight pause.

Three days later.

Jill   The day I was confirmed . . . Father Vianney gave me a Bible. On the front page there was a painting of heaven. All fluffy clouds and angels. On the back page . . . hell. Do you know what hell is, Ollie? *Do* you?

Ollie   . . . Jill, I –

Jill   It's fire. That's all. It's burning in fire for all eternity. Imagine that. No morphine. No relief. Just pain and screaming. For ever.

Slight pause.

Ollie   A week later. I've just seen Mitch and Brandy. They said The Never Enough Shopping Centre is starting a shopping channel. Mitch and Brandy are going to apply to be presenters. I think they stand a good chance. Brandy wants your advice about what to wear for the interview. She says you two haven't had a good chat for ages. You should go over and –

Jill   And what? Let slip our sofa's growing a beard?

Ollie   You . . . you *won't* do that.

Jill   How d'you *know*?

Ollie   . . . Jill –

Jill   I feel this . . . thing inside me. Just here. Next to my
heart. It's small. The size of sparrow. I don't know what it
looks like. But I know it's got claws because it scratches. And
I imagine it to be dark blue – mauve almost – like the veins
on my mum's hands. I hear it talking. Its voice is high
pitched and screeching. It's talking about all the things we've
done. It talks a lot at night – sometimes so loud I'm
surprised it doesn't wake you – but mostly . . . mostly it talks
when I'm with other people. I can feel it clawing its way up
my throat – its voice getting louder and louder – and it takes
all my will power – every atom of it – to keep this creature
silent.

Ollie   . . . Okay . . . This is what I think you should do. Go
over and see Brandy. Stay there for as long as you can. But
the moment the scratching and screeching starts becoming
too much . . . you come back here. Tomorrow – see her
again. Try to stay a bit longer. The next day – a bit longer.
Keep doing that. Until the scratching and screeching stops.
Okay?

Jill   Okay.

Slight pause.

She walks off.

He starts looking round at everyone.

He's trying to say something.

The words won't come.

He keeps trying –

Jill (*calling off*)   Ollie?!

Ollie   It's five weeks later.

Jill (*calling, off*) Ollie?!

Ollie   I'm in the nursery.

Jill *appears.*

Jill   What're you doing?

Ollie   Looking at the Celestial Enhancer Whatsit.

Jill   Is your brain getting bigger?

Ollie   I don't know about that. It's certainly aching a bit.

Jill   I've got some news –

Ollie   Where's Benjy?

Jill   I left him with Brandy – What's my Bible doing here?

Ollie   I've been reading it.

Jill   *You?!*

Ollie   What's the dictionary definition of a miracle?

Jill   Wh-what?

Ollie   Miracle. Dictionary definition?

Jill   I . . . I'm not sure . . .

Ollie   'A wonderful supernatural event.'

Jill   Ollie –

Ollie   Now, I've always believed the universe is full of wonderful *natural* events. But *super*natural ? Never.

Jill   I don't know where all this –

Ollie   The renovations, Jill. *They* are without doubt wonderful supernatural events. Well, *aren't* they. *Eh*?

Jill   Yes . . . I suppose they –

Ollie   So if miracles *are* possible then . . .

Jill   Then?

Ollie   Then . . . everything in the Bible . . .

Jill   . . . I'm having a baby.

He stares.

Jill I did sort of half suspect. But there was so much going on in my head and . . . The way I was behaving . . . Yana's been insisting I see my doctor for weeks. So has Miriam. Brandy took me there this afternoon. Ollie, I've been suffering from post-conception depression. That's what it's been. But now . . . I'm fine . . . Will you kiss me please?

He kisses her.

Jill This nursery will have to be re-done. And we'll need a new pram. A big one to fit both Benjy and his brother.

Ollie 'Brother –?' You mean – ?

Jill It's a boy, yes.

Ollie Two boys! Yesss! – I mean a girl would have been great too but . . . you know.

Jill Mmm.

Ollie We'll have to start thinking of a name.

Jill I already have. Daniel.

Ollie . . . Dad would be . . . he'd be . . .

They embrace.

Jill Oh! I nearly forgot. More news!

Ollie More?!

Jill I've just met our new neighbour.

Ollie Number five's been sold?!

Jill His name's Larry. You'll like him. He's single. Been working on cruise ships for the past fifteen years. 'I've been round the world so many times I feel like a satellite, my lovely.' He's in 'showbiz'. Compère or something. He loved little Benjy. I told him it was Benjy's first birthday next week. Larry asked if we were having a party. I said no but . . . now I think about it . . .

Ollie You think we should.

Jill   I think we should.

Ollie   I think we should too.

Jill   Oh, Ollie, it'll be our first party on Gilead Close. We'll make it –

Ollie and **Jill**   A birthday party no one will *ever* forget! – 'Where's the party!?'

Ollie   Out here, you two!

Jill   In the garden!

Jill and **Ollie**   'Ooo!'

Jill   Hello, Brand.

Ollie   Hello, Mitch.

Jill   'Oh, it looks amazing – Doesn't it, Mitch?'

Ollie   'It does, Brand – Look at all that food!'

Jill   'You could feed the third world with that lot!'

Ollie   'You've put lights in the bushes, mate!' Wait till it gets dark, Mitch – Magic!

Jill   'Ooo, I want it to be dark now! *Now!*'

Ollie   'Patience, Brand.'

Jill   Would you like something to drink? 'Ooo, yes, please.'

Ollie   We've made some punch.

Jill   Benjy Birthday Special. 'Ooo, that sounds scrummy – Don't it, Mitch?'

Ollie   'It does, Brand.' I'll get you some. 'Thanks, mate.' No, problem, Mitch.

Jill   'Where's birthday boy?' Under the tree, Brand

Ollie   On his new blanket.

Jill   His *birthday* blanket.

Ollie It's got 'Happy Birthday' written on it.

Jill and **Ollie** 'Nwahhh.'

Jill 'Happy birthday, Benjy-wenjy. Oh, he's so cute – Don't you think so, Mitch?'

Ollie 'Super cute, Brand.'

Jill 'We've got him a little something.' Oh, you shouldn't have. 'Of *course* we should – Shouldn't we, Mitch?'

Ollie 'Of *course* we should, Brand.'

Jill 'It's just a toy.'

Ollie 'It's called The Pop Up Dinosaur Smasher.'

Jill 'Pop Up Dinosaur Activity *Toy* actually.'

Ollie 'There's a row of eggs.'

Jill '*Dinosaur* eggs.'

Ollie 'All different colours.'

Jill 'And dinosaurs pop out of the eggs.'

Ollie 'Now . . . there's a row of coloured buttons along the front.'

Jill 'Each one a colour of one of the eggs.'

Ollie 'And here's a hammer.'

Jill 'A dinosaur bone actually.'

Ollie 'Not a *real* dinosaur bone.'

Jill 'Unless dinosaurs were made of plastic – ha, ha!'

Ollie 'Ha, ha!'

Jill Ha, ha!

Ollie Ha, ha! – Here's your drinks.

Jill 'Ooo, thank you, Ollie.'

Ollie   'Thanks, mate.'

Jill   'Now . . . when Benjy sees a *red* dinosaur hatch –'

Ollie   'He smashes the *red* button with the bone.'

Jill   'And the red baby dinosaur –'

Ollie   'Goes back in its egg.'

Jill   'And when the yellow dinosaurs hatches –'

Ollie   'Yellow – Smash!'

Jill   'And the dinosaurs keep trying to hatch until –'

Ollie   'Smash! Smash!'

Jill   'All the dinosaurs are back in their eggs at the same time.'

Ollie   'And when that happens –'

Jill and **Ollie**   'DA-DAH!'

Jill   'A white angel pops up behind them.'

Ollie   'Er . . . it's not a white angel, Brand.'

Jill   'Er . . . I believe it is, Mitch.'

Ollie   'No, no, it's a cloud.'

Jill   'A cloud'?

Ollie   Of *course*! Caused by the comet – Right, Mitch? 'Right, mate.'

Jill   'What comet?'

Ollie and **Jill**   'Hello, there?!'

Ollie   Nish!

Jill   Yana!

Ollie   'Oh, you've made the garden look wonderful.'

Jill   'Have you ever seen so much food?"

Ollie 'Enough to feed the third world.'

Jill 'That's what I said – Didn't I, Mitch?'

Ollie 'You did, Brand.'

Jill Would you both like something to drink?

Ollie 'They've made some special punch.'

Jill 'Benjy Birthday Special.'

Ollie 'We think it's scrummy – Don't we, Brand?'

Jill 'We do, Mitch.'

Ollie 'Well, who can refuse that? – Where's our Navneet got to?'

Jill 'He couldn't've gone far, Nish.'

Ollie 'He was right behind us.'

Jill 'There's lights in the bushes. You see?'

Ollie 'Did you do all that, Ollie.' I did, Nish.

Jill 'He's Mr DIY – Right, Mitch?'

Ollie 'Right, Brand.'

Jill 'We're waiting for the dark.'

Ollie 'Your're waiting for the dark?' All the lights – they look magical at night.

Jill 'Oh, let's enjoy the sunshine first.' Yes, we've been so lucky with the weather – Haven't we, Ollie?

Ollie Hottest day of the year so far.

Jill 'Someone up there likes you.'

Ollie Wh-what's that supposed to mean?

Jill It's just a saying, sweetheart. 'Have I said something wrong?' Of course not – Nish and Yana's drinks, sweetheart?

Ollie Oh . . . yes. Sorry – Do you want another one?

Jill   No, thank you.

Ollie   I think *I* might.

Jill   'Now where's the birthday boy?' He's over there, Yana.

Ollie   Our little man's under the tree.

Jill   'On his cute new blanket?'

Ollie   'It says "Happy Birthday" – Don't it, Brand?'

Jill   'It does, Mitch. He's playing with the toy we gave him.'

Ollie   'We have brought him a gift too.'

Jill   Oh, you shouldn't have.

Ollie   'Indeed we should.'

Jill   'It's nothing really.'

Ollie   'A baby beanie.'

Jill   'Ooo, it's so cute!' – That's very kind of you both – Ollie?

Ollie   Very kind. Thank you.

Jill   'A baby beanie is always useful.'

Ollie   'It'll keep Benjy's head warm in the winter.'

Jill   'And the sun off it in the summer.'

Ollie   'A day like today. Phew!'

Jill   'Shall I put it on him?' Well . . . he's in the shade now, Yana. 'Not *totally* in the shade, Jill.' 'Oh, put it on, put it on, Yana! – Mitch! Photo!'

Ollie   'You got it, Brand.'

Jill   'Happy birthday, dear little Benjy . . . There!'

Ollie and **Jill**   'Nwahhhh.'

Ollie   'BANG!'

Jill and **Ollie**   AHHHH! 'NAVNEET!'

Jill 'Stop firing that stupid gun.'

Ollie 'Why should I – BANG!'

Jill and **Ollie** AHHHH! 'NAVNEET!'

Jill 'We should never have got it for him.'

Ollie 'It's an expensive toy – Right, Brand?'

Jill 'Right, Mitch.'

Ollie 'Say happy birthday to baby Ben –' 'BANG!'

Jill 'Enough, Navneet!'

Ollie 'That is *not* polite.'

Jill 'Ooo, is that . . . blood? – Mitch?'

Ollie 'A digital projection of some kind – Right, Nish?' 'Yes, yes, Mitch. It has three levels of splatter.'

Jill 'Oh, I feel a bit queasy.'

Ollie Your drinks, Nish, Yana.

Jill 'Thank you, Ollie.'

Ollie 'Thank you, Ollie.' – 'BANG!'

Jill and **Ollie** AHHHH! 'NAVNEET!'

Jill 'Stop killing!'

Ollie Killing?!

Jill Are you alright?

Ollie Of *course* I'm alright.

Jill 'Hello, there, hello!' Hello, there, Miriam.

Ollie Hello, Miriam.

Jill 'Jill, Ollie. Hello, Brand, Mitch.'

Ollie 'Hey, there.'

Jill 'Hey, there.' 'Yana, Nish.'

Ollie   'Hello.'

Jill   'Hello.' 'Say hello, Jonathan.'

Ollie   'Hell . . . Hell . . . ' He's saying 'hell'.

Jill   Of *course* he's not. 'Is something wrong?' Not at all, Miriam. 'Oh, the garden looks just gorgeous – Doesn't it, Jonny?'

Ollie   'Hell –' Hell again.

Jill   Stop it! Can Ollie get you both a drink? 'They've made some punch.'

Ollie   'Hello.'

Jill   Hello, Jonathan. Punch for you? – Ollie?

Ollie   Eh? Oh. It's called Benjy Birthday Special, Jonathan.

Jill   'We both think it's scrummy – Don't we, Mitch?'

Ollie   'We do, Brand.'

Jill   'Do you think it's scrummy, Yana?' 'Yes, I do.' 'Do you think it's scrummy, Nish?'

Ollie   'Very scrummy, Brandy.'

Jill   'We *all* think it's scrummy!' 'Well, who can refuse that?' 'That's what Nish said – ha, ha.' 'Ha, ha.'

Ollie   'Ha, ha.'

Jill   Ha, ha – Ollie?

Ollie   Scrummy drinks coming up!

Jill   'And look at all that food. Enough to feed the third world.'

Ollie   'That's what Brand said – Wasn't it, Brand?'

Jill   'It was, Mitch. And Nish said it too.'

Ollie and **Jill**   'We all keep saying the same things – ha, ha!'

Ollie 'Ha, ha!'

Jill 'Ha, ha!' – 'Where *have* the twins got to?'

Ollie I can see them in the lounge, Miriam.

Jill 'What on earth are they – ? TRISTAN! TINA!'

Ollie and **Jill** 'What?'

Jill 'Come out here!'

Ollie and **Jill** 'We're looking at stuff.'

Jill 'Here! Now! – I'm sorry, Jill.' What for? We've got nothing to hide – Have we, Ollie?

Ollie What?

Jill Nothing to hide.

Ollie No. Who said we had?

Jill *No one* said we had – Where're those drinks?

Ollie Coming, coming – Do you want one, sweetheart?

Jill No. And nor should you.

Ollie I think I should.

Jill I think you –

Ollie 'BANG!'

Ollie and **Jill** AHHHH! 'NAVNEET!'

Jill Oh, hello, Tristan. Tina. 'Decided to join us, have you?'

Ollie 'There's lots of new stuff in the house.'

Jill 'New telly.'

Ollie 'New floorboards.'

Jill 'New ornaments.'

Ollie 'New painting on the wall.'

Jill 'Oh, I noticed that. Expensive frame.'

Ollie 'It's *all* expensive.'

Jill 'And you've got more tropical fish.'

Ollie 'Aquariums are *so* disgusting.'

Jill 'They're marine concentration camps.' 'Enough! Stop being disagreeable and say hello to our hosts.'

Ollie and **Jill**   'Hello to our hosts.'

Ollie 'BANG!'

Ollie and **Jill**   AHHHH! 'NAVNEET!'

Ollie Your drink, Miriam.

Jill 'Thank you.'

Ollie Jonathan. 'Th-thank –'

Jill 'How much money did your parents leave you?'

Ollie 'It must've been a fortune.'

Jill 'Was it diamond mine in the Congo or something?'

Ollie 'They use slave labour in diamond mines.'

Jill 'If a miner runs away they set the dogs on him.'

Ollie 'They chop his toes off.'

Jill 'Stop this nonsense – Tell them, Jonathan.'

Ollie 'St-st-st –'

Jill 'You heard your father! – Now, where's our birthday boy?'

Ollie Our little man's over there.

Jill Under the tree. 'He's on his cute new blanket.'

Ollie 'His cute new birthday blanket.'

Jill 'It says "Happy Birthday" on it.'

Ollie 'He's playing with the toy we gave him.'

Jill   'Hello, Benjamin – Oh, very sensible to put something on his head, Jill.' 'That's *our* present.' 'Very sensible, Yana.' 'Look at him smash those dinosaurs – Mitch, Mitch! Photo!'

Ollie   'You got it, Brand!'

Jill   'We've brought him a gift too.' 'Oh, you shouldn't have, Miriam.' 'Nonsense, nonsense – Jonny?'

Ollie   'Here –'

Jill   'A silver spoon.'

Ollie and **Jill**   'Oooo!'

Jill   'We've had his name engraved. You see?' That's very thoughtful – Isn't it, Ollie?

Ollie   Yes, it is.

Jill and Ollie   'Elitist crap.'

Jill   Would either of you delightful twins like a sandwich?

Ollie   'No way!'

Jill   'Tristan!'

Ollie   'Look what's in them, Mum!'

Jill   'Ham.'

Ollie   'Bacon.'

Jill   Not *all* of them.

Ollie   '*Most* of them.'

Jill   'It's a pig holocaust.' 'Oh, that's a disgraceful thing to say.'

Ollie   Carnivores are disgraceful people.

Jill   'Meat is murder, Mum.'

Ollie   Murder?!

Jill   'Yes, murder.'

Ollie 'Murder.'

Jill Ollie. You okay?

Ollie What? Yes.

Jill You're trembling a bit.

Ollie I'm not.

Jill You are, sweetheart.

Ollie 'Have you seen how they kill pigs?'

Jill 'I'm sure it's humane, Tristan.' 'It's not humane at all, Mum.' But . . . but don't they electrocute them first? – Ollie?'

Ollie Of *course* they do. 'You think that's painless?'

Jill Of *course* it's painless – Ollie?

Ollie Electrocution is *totally* painless.

Jill 'It's not painless at all.'

Ollie 'Not at all.'

Jill 'It hurts.'

Ollie 'It hurts like hell.'

Jill 'You should hear them squeal.'

Ollie 'It's horrible.'

Jill and **Ollie** 'EEEEE!'

Ollie Shut up!

Jill Ollie! – 'You've upset our host now.'

Jill and **Ollie** 'Good.'

Ollie 'COO-EEE!'

Jill Larry!

Ollie 'I'm late, I'm late, sorry.'

Jill You're not late at all.

Ollie   'I've been rehearsing my song.'

Jill   Larry's going to sing for us.

Ollie   'It's my birthday gift – Greetings, one and all.'

Jill   'Hey, Larry.'

Ollie   'Hey, Larry.'

Jill   'Afternoon, Larry.'

Ollie   'Afternoon, Larry.'

Jill   'Hello, Larry.'

Ollie   'Hell . . . Hell . . .' He's doing it *again*!

Jill   Stop being ridiculous.

Ollie   Hell!

Jill   'Is something wrong?' Nothing at all, Miriam.

Ollie   'Are you all sweltering in this heat, my lovelies, or is it me?'

Jill   'It's tropical weather, Larry.'

Ollie   'Hottest day of the year so far.'

Jill   'In a garden short of shade.' 'It's a Mediterranean-style garden – Right, Jill.' Moroccan-style, yes, Brand. 'Well, there's usually more shade in a Moroccan garden.' There *is* shade, Miriam. And it's *all* where Benjy is.

Ollie   'Where *is* the birthday boy? I can't see –'

Jill   Under the tree, Larry. 'On his cute new blanket.'

Ollie   'His birthday blanket.'

Jill   'It says "Happy Birthday" on it. You see?'

Ollie   'He's playing with the toy we bought him.'

Jill   'It's about the battle between dinosaurs and angels.'

Ollie   'Er . . . that's not what it's about, Brand.'

Jill 'Er . . . I believe it is, Mitch.' 'We bought him the beanie.'

Ollie 'Good idea in this heat, Yana.'

Jill 'That's what I said.'

Ollie 'Hottest day of the year.'

Jill He's in the shade, Nish.

Ollie 'Sunstroke, Jill.'

Jill 'It happens very easily, Jill.'

Ollie '*Very* easily, Jill.'

Jill He won't get sunstroke because he *is* in the bloody shade. 'Not *totally* in the shade.' 'You don't want him to get burnt.'

Ollie Burnt? Who said 'burnt'?

Jill Miriam did. It's nothing, sweetheart.

Ollie 'A burn is *not* nothing, my lovely.'

Jill Can Ollie get you a drink, Larry? 'They've made some punch.'

Ollie 'It's Benjy Birthday Special.'

Jill 'We think it's scrummy – Don't we, Mitch?'

Ollie 'We do, Brand. So do you, don't you and Yana, don't you. Nish?' 'We do – Don't we, Yana?'

Jill 'We do – So do you and Jonathan, don't you, Miriam.' 'We do – Don't we, Jonny.'

Ollie Y-yes!

Jill How can you refuse a glass now, Larry?

Ollie 'No alcohol before a performance, I'm afraid.'

Jill Oh . . . well, would you like some juice? – Ollie?

Ollie We . . . we've got pineapple. And tropical fruit.

Jill 'They've got everything.'

Ollie 'Every juice in the world.'

Jill 'Stop it, you two.'

Ollie BANG!

Ollie and **Jill** AHHHH! 'NAVNEET!' 'EEEEE!'

Ollie 'No sudden noises please. My heart – a tad dodgy.'

Jill Oh, Larry, I'm sorry.

Ollie 'It's nothing. So long as I'm not scared to death.'

Jill 'You hear that, Navneet?'

Ollie 'Do not kill the guests!' Killing again.

Jill Ollie!

Ollie 'I do believe he's had one too many drinks, my lovely.'

Jill 'He's punch drunk with the punch he's drunk – ha, ha.'

Ollie Oh, very good, Brand – ha, ha.

Jill Ha, ha.

Ollie Ha, ha.

Jill Ha, ha.

Ollie 'Ha, ha.'

Jill So what would you like, Larry?

Ollie 'What's that, my lovely?'

Jill To drink.

Ollie Oh, I'd kill for a cup of tea.' Kill?

Jill   Shush! 'Ooo, Ollie's a bit tipsy.' 'Alcohol and sunshine.' 'Not a good mix, Miriam.' 'A Moroccan garden with no Moroccan shade.' There *is* shade! 'Well, *I* can't see it. Can *you* see it, Yana? 'No, I can't see it, Miriam.' Sweetheart, will you . . . will you please get Larry his tea?

Ollie   Wh-what?

Jill   *Tea*! *Larry*!

Ollie   Oh . . . yes.

Jill   Milk and sugar, Larry?

Ollie   'Just lemon please, my lovely.'

Jill   Earl Grey?

Ollie   'Heavenly.'

Jill   'Slave labour's "heavenly" is it?'

Ollie   'Slave labour?'

Jill   'People on tea plantations.'

Ollie   'Picking your tea.'

Jill   'Children mostly.'

Ollie   'Their fingers get infected.'

Jill   'They have them amputated.'

Ollie   'Is that worth your "heavenly" cuppa?' 'Lordy, you two are a bundle of laughs.'

Jill   'You're spoiling the party for everyone.'

Ollie   'No, no, Miriam. They're amusing. Have you ever thought of going into show business, my lovelies?'

Jill and **Ollie**   'Don't patronise us!'

Ollie   'Answer the question!' 'Very well. Does the idea of children with severed fingers bother me? Of course it does. But believe me, when you've been going round the world for fifteen years – and seen as much as I have – you witness things that'll bother you in every port of call. At first – when you're young – you want to do something about it. All problems are black and white. The solution must be simple. But the more you witness – and the more . . . mature you get – you begin to realise most problems are not simple at all. There's no black. No white. Why, there's not even grey. Most problems are . . . purple with yellow spots. Or . . . orange with green squiggles. What you eventually learn to do is . . . appreciate the pattern, not worry about the problem.'

Ollie   'BANG!'

Ollie and **Jill**   AHHHH! 'NAVNEET!' 'EEEEE!'

Ollie   Your tea, Larry. 'No human fingers in it, I trust.' 'Human – ? Wh-what?

Jill   It's nothing – Shhh!

Ollie   But he said –

Jill   Ollie! 'Ooo, Ollie's a bit tipsy.' 'Alcohol and sunshine.' 'Dangerous.' 'Deadly.'

Ollie   Dead? – 'BANG!'

Ollie and **Jill**   AHHHH! 'NAVNEET!' 'EEEEE!'

Ollie   Shut up!

Jill   Ollie!

Ollie   'Ladies and gentlemen, perhaps I may be the one to propose a toast.'

Jill   'Ooo, yes, Larry!'

Ollie   'Go for it, mate.'

Jill   Please do, Larry

Ollie   'My dear neighbours and friends. We are here today – in the wonderful home of Ollie and Jill – to celebrate the first birthday of their beautiful boy Benjamin. May he always be surrounded with as much love as he is today. Happy birthday, Benjamin.'

Ollie and **Jill**   Happy birthday, Benjamin.

They drink.

Ollie   'And now . . . my little song. And I should tell you I sing this as – and I don't want to steal any of our beloved Benjy's thunder –'

Jill   'Hard to steal thunder on a day like this.' 'Hottest day of the year so far.' 'In a Moroccan garden with no Moroccan shade.' What were you about to say, Larry?

Ollie   'Well . . . you are all looking at the new manager of light entertainment for The Never Enough Shopping Centre.'

They cheer and clap, etc.

Jill   'Oh! Mitch! Shall we tell them? *Shall* we?'

Ollie   'Let's *do* it, Brand!'

Jill   'We weren't going to say anything –'

Ollie   'Because we only heard this morning –'

Jill   'And *we* didn't want to steal any of Beny-wenjy's thunder either but –'

Ollie   '*We* are the new presenters of –'

Jill   '– The Never Enough Shopping Centre –'

Ollie   '– Shopping Channel.'

Jill and Ollie   'Because enough is never enough.'

They cheer and clap, etc.

Ollie   'Well, if we're *all* stealing a little bit of thunder . . . shall we, Yana?'

Jill   'I think we might as well, Nish.'

Ollie   'Me and Yana are starting a cosmetic surgery clinic in The Never Enough Shopping Centre.'

They cheer and clap, etc.

Jill   'Well, while there's still some thunder left to steal.' Not you too, Miriam. 'A small antique shop on the top floor. '

They all cheer and clap, etc.

Ollie   'Oh, what a wonderfully emotional moment, my lovelies. It makes the song I'm about to sing even more fitting because – and you all are the first to hear the news – it will be the official theme music for The Never Enough Shopping Centre.'

They cheer and clap.

Ollie   'Make it bigger, make it brighter –' It's our song!

Jill   We don't *own* it, Ollie.

Ollie   'Make it faster, make it brighter.'

But we sung it when – You remember when we sung it?

Jill   Of *course* I do.

Ollie   'Make it stand out in the crowdier –' He knows something, Jill.

Jill   Don't talk rubbish.

Ollie   I *know* he knows.

Jill   'What's that, Jill?' Oh . . . Ollie says he knows this song, Miriam. 'Oh, so do I – Make it hipper, make it hotter.'

Ollie   'That's it, my lovelies! Join in!' Jill! Everyone here suspects something. I can *feel* it!

Jill   They *don't*, Ollie.

Ollie and **Jill**   'Hell, I still want more.'

They clap.

Jill   . . . '*How* did they die?'

Ollie   Wh-what?

Jilll   'Your parents.'

Ollie   'These parents who left you lots and lots of money.'

Jill   'Now, that is *really* enough, you two.'

Ollie   'I think I'll have my birthday punch now.'

Jill   You deserve it, Larry – Ollie?

Ollie   'Your parents couldn't've been very old.'

Jill   'So how come they're dead?'

Ollie   Dead?

Jill   'What's wrong with Ollie?' Nothing's wrong with him, Miriam. 'But he's shaking and –' Nothing's *wrong* with him!

Ollie   'How did they die?'

Jill   What?

Ollie   'Your *parents*.'

Jill   It was an accident.

Ollie   'What *sort* of accident?'

Jill   A traffic accident.

Ollie   'They were hit by a car?'

Jill   No.

Ollie   'They were *in* a car?'

Jill   Yes.

Ollie   'I'm gasping here, my lovely.'

Jill   Where's Larry's drink got to, sweetheart? 'You're gasping because of the sun.'

Ollie   'It does seem to be getting hotter, Yana.'

Jill 'Should you move baby inside, Jill.' Benjy's just fine, Yana.

Ollie 'BANG!'

Ollie and **Jill** AHHHH! 'NAVNEET!' 'EEEEE!'

Ollie 'How did it happen?'

Jill Wh-what?

Ollie 'The car accident.'

Jill It . . . it was a freak thing – Larry's drink, sweetheart!

Ollie 'I'm about to pass out here, my lovely.'

Jill 'It's the heat.' 'Ooo, I'm catching the sun a bit! Look! – Are you, Mitch?'

Ollie 'I am, Brand.'

Jill 'The *baby* is too.' No, he's *not*. 'Yes, he *is*.' No, he's *not*. 'So what happened?' Eh?

Ollie 'This *freak* accident.'

Jill Oh! They were – 'You don't have to tell them, Jill.' I don't mind, Miriam –

Ollie 'BANG!'

Ollie and **Jill** AHHHH! 'NAVNEET!' 'EEEEE!'

Jill My mum and Ollie's dad – they'd been on holiday.

Ollie 'Together?'

Jill Yes.

Ollie 'Were they a couple?'

Jill No. But . . . well, my mum had helped Ollie's dad with a problem.

Ollie 'What problem?'

Jill 'Don't pry.' It's alright, Miriam. A drinking problem. She introduced him to Alcoholics Anonymous. He got better and – as a thank you present – he took her somewhere she'd always wanted to visit.

Ollie 'Where'd he take her?'

Jill Lourdes.

Ollie 'Where's that?'

Jill France. 'It's supposed to have healing waters, is that right?' That's right, Yana.

Ollie Your drink, Larry. 'Thank you, my lovely.' 'Was your mum ill, then?

Jill 'Is that why she wanted 'healing waters'?'

Ollie Jill's mum had arthritis.

Jill Rheumatoid arthritis.

Ollie She was on morphine.

Jill 'So . . . she believed the Lourdes bullshit, did she – ha,ha, ha!'

Ollie It is *not* bullshit! Her arthritis healed – Didn't it, Jill?

Jill It did, yes.

Ollie She phoned us.

Jill The swelling had gone.

Ollie She wasn't it pain anymore. 'Tell us about this freak accident!'

Jill They were in a minicab.

Ollie On their way to the airport.

Jill And . . . a bird flew in.

Ollie 'Into the minicab?'

Jill Yes. 'That can't happen.'

Ollie   Well, it obviously fucking can.

Jill   'Well, really.' 'Language.' 'He's so tipsy.' 'The heat.'

Ollie   'Hottest day of the year so far.'

Jill   'A Moroccan garden with no Moroccan shade.'

Ollie   'Was the minicab driver killed?

Jill   No.

Ollie   'BANG!'

Ollie and **Jill**   AHHHH! 'NAVNEET!' 'EEEEE!'

Jill   So . . . your mum had this so-called miraculous cure.'

Ollie   Don't say 'so called', you little shit.

Jill   'Well, really.' 'Language.' 'He's *so* tipsy.' 'Alcohol and heat.'

Ollie   'And then . . . Flap, flap.'

Jill   'Crash, crash.'

Ollie   'Shall I get Benjy something to drink, my lovely?

Jill   'The poor thing must be getting very parched, Jill?' The baby's bloody fine, thank you, Miriam.

Ollie   'How did that make you feel?'

Jill   What?

Ollie   'Flap, flap.'

Jill   'Crash, crash.'

Ollie   'You're religious, right?'

Jill   I . . . yes.

Ollie   'Didn't you *wonder* – ?'

Jill   'Why did God *do* that?'

Ollie   'Where's the *meaning*?'

Jill 'Didn't you . . . *doub*t?'

Ollie 'BANG!'

Ollie and **Jill** AHHHH! 'NAVNEET!' 'EEEEE!'

Jill 'I'll move him.' Wh-what? 'Come to your Auntie Miriam, Benjamin.' Don't you *dare* touch him. 'He'll burn here, Jill.'

Ollie Burn?

Jill *No one* is going to burn.

Ollie 'BANG!'

Ollie and **Jill** AHHHH! 'NAVNEET!' 'EEEEE!'

Jill 'It's far the best, Jill.' Don't you lay a hand on him. 'But he can so easily burn.'

Ollie 'BANG!'

Jill and **Ollie** 'AHHH!' 'NAVNEET!' 'EEEEEEEE!'

Jill 'And if anything *did* happen to him –' 'You'd never forgive yourselves, would you – Oliver?'

Ollie No. We'd never . . . we'd never forgive ourselves . . . Never . . .

Jill Sweetheart?

Ollie We'll never be forgiven – We're . . . we're going to hell!

Jill 'Ooo, what . . . is something wrong?' 'It's most certainly sunstroke – Yana?' 'Has all the symptoms, Miriam.' 'He's gone totally bonkers.'

Ollie We're going to hell! I know we are! We're going to burn and burn for ever and they'll be no morphine and we'll scream and –

Jill Shhh, Ollie. No, no.

He collapses.

Ollie   We're going to hell . . . We're going to hell . . . We're going to hell . . .

He curls into ball, whimpering.

Jill   Would you . . . would you all go now, please . . . The party's over . . . Yes, yes, Ollie's fine . . . He's been working very hard and . . . Yes, yes, just go . . . Bye. Thank you all for your lovely presents . . . Bye . . . Bye . . .

Pause.

Well . . . that brings us almost up to where we began, everyone. The party – that was this afternoon. It took me nearly three hours – not to mention a big pot of coffee – to get Ollie back to normal. Well, as normal as you ever get, eh, sweetheart?

He doesn't respond.

Jill   Oh, Ollie, are you okay? – Sorry, everyone, all these emotions are so . . . so recent – Sweetheart? The neighbours have gone. We're with friends now. Remember?

Ollie   I . . . yeah . . . sorry, everyone.

Gradually stands.

A bit too much Meisner technique there – ha, ha! Okay. So. When I finally came back to my senses –

Jill   Sobered up.

Ollie   That too. Jill and me – we had a long talk about things.

Jill   Once more, we can't tell you everything.

Ollie   But all came down to one thing.

Jill   Confession.

Ollie   You see, most people's idea of confession –

Jill   The box. The priest.

Ollie   That's *not* how it started. It *used* to be standing in front of your community and *explaining* what you'd done.

Jill   It wasn't about *forgiveness* as such.

Ollie   It was about making everyone *understand* –

Jill   And if everyone – the community – could *understand* –

Ollie   Then . . . that was okay.

Jill   And so we thought –

Ollie   If we could do that –

Jill   If we could make ourselves understood –

Ollie   To a group of people –

Jill   Who would listen without prejudice.

Ollie   Then it might stop . . .

Jill   What happened this afternoon –

Ollie   Ever happening again.

Jill   To Ollie . . . or me.

Ollie   And then . . . you all started appearing.

Jill   Out of nowhere.

Ollie   Like you'd all just walked in off the street.

Jill   And so we started working out how to tell you.

Ollie   Why we did.

Jill   What we did.

Ollie   And now we have.

Jill   And we want to ask you –

Ollie   Do you understand?

Jill   Or to put it another way –

Ollie   Would you do the same?

Jill   Don't worry. We're not going to take a vote.

Ollie   We just want you to think about it for a moment.

Jill   Ponder the . . .

Ollie   The possibilities.

Jill   You could have the house you always wanted.

Ollie   Fill it with the stuff you always wanted.

Jill   Isn't having all that worth the lives of a few homeless people.

Ollie   You walk past them every day.

Jill   Do you worry about them when it's freezing?

Ollie   Would you bring them into your home to feed them?

Jill   Have you *ever* done that?

Ollie   Even though you know they might well die out there.

Jill   Every winter.

Ollie   Hundreds.

Jill   All the time.

Ollie   So wouldn't those freezing nobodies be better off –

Jill   As a coffee table

Ollie   Or lawnmower.

Jill   We're not going to take a vote.

Ollie   We'll know what you're thinking –

Jill   By the looks on your faces

Ollie   Go on.

Jill   Ponder . . .

Pause.

They agree!

Ollie   Oh, thank you, everyone.

Jill   Thank you.

Ollie   I feel so relieved.

Jill   Me too.

Ollie   We can carry on as normal.

Jill   No guilt.

Ollie   None! I want a sauna in the cellar.

Jill   I want a new buggy for Benjy.

Ollie   I want golf clubs.

Jill   I want – Oh! What's that?

Ollie   Sounds like the letterbox.

Jill   Too late for the postman.

Ollie   Hand delivered. Hand written . . . It's from Larry. His letterhead. (*Reading.*) 'Dear Ollie and Jill, I speak on behalf of all your neighbours when I say thank you for a most diverting birthday party.'

Jill   I despise sarcasm.

Ollie   'All of us returned to my humble abode after we had been summarily dismissed for some afternoon aperitifs and conversation.'

Jill   Oh, he's so pompous. Honestly.

Ollie   'We all decided to inform you of what we have been discussing and it was agreed that I should be the one to write the letter what I am now doing.'

Jill   Illiterate too.

Ollie   'It has come to our attention that your behaviour is putting the value of this property "hot spot" at risk.'

Jill   *What*?!

Takes letter from him.

Jill 'Namely, your persistence in bringing vagrants back to your house. I myself have not seen it but I have been assured by all the others – especially Brandy and Mitch – this has been a regular feature of your life here. May I remind you, these vagrants are not only potential robbers and murderers – it baffles all of us that, with a baby in the house, you would do this – but they are also potential carriers of God knows what diseases. Is it any wonder you have discovered mice in your house.

Ollie Jesus!

Jill To conclude, by helping the homeless – not to mention some of the eccentric behaviour on display at your own child's birthday party – your are bringing the value of our houses down. This must stop forthwith.'

Ollie 'Forthwith'?

Jill From now on we are instigating a Neighbourhood Watch. We are setting up CCTV cameras. And we would be grateful if you would sign the enclosed contract to state your agreement and participation –

He snatches letter and tears it up.

Ollie That's what I think of their fucking contract! *We* created *everything* here! The whole fucking neighbourhood. Jesus, they wouldn't even *have* The Never Enough fucking Shopping Centre if it wasn't for *us*. We're going to carry on with the renovations and they can go to fucking hell.

Slight pause.

We can't do any more renovations, can we?

Jill I don't see how. They'll be watching us all the time.

Miss Dee Hello, children.

Jill and **Ollie** Miss Dee!

Ollie   How did you – ?

Miss Dee   Your front door was open. Oh! Look at this house! What a wonder! You two are my prize pupils and no mistake.

Jill   But Miss Dee –

Miss Dee   I know, I know. That *silly* letter. Something like this always happens. The people who get the regeneration started – their way of achieving it starts sticking out like a toddler's leg from the jaws of a crocodile. Clause Six, subsection six. Remember?

Jill   'The signatories must maintain discretion.'

Miss Dee   That is why we have reached . . . 'the moment'.

Jill   'The moment'?

Miss Dee   'The moment' where you have to make a decision. To stay. Or . . . move on.

Slight pause.

I have a new contract for you here.

Ollie   Another house?

Jill   Like this one was?

Miss Dee   The contract is exactly the same, yes.

Ollie   With the same . . . perks?

Miss Dee   'Perks'? Honestly, child, I've no idea what you mean.

Jill   He means we'll have to renovate . . . like we did this one.

Miss Dee   Well, if you can make the new house look as wonderful as this, you'll make your Miss Dee so very proud.

Jill   I want to do it, Ollie. I want more things. Better things.

Ollie   Me too.

Reaches for contract.

Miss Dee   A friendly warning . . . With each new house, it sometimes feels the sacrifices we have to make . . . double.

Ollie   'Double'?

Miss Dee   Double.

Ollie   Miss Dee . . . can me and Jill talk this through for a moment please?

Miss Dee   Of course, of course.

Jill *and* **Ollie** *go to one side.*

Ollie   You know what she's saying?

Jill   Each renovation will need *two* renovators.

Ollie   That's a *lot* of renovators, Jill.

Jill   We need to find a way of making it work, Ollie. We can't stay here and never renovate again. That's just not an option. You *know* that?

Ollie   I know, I know . . . Okay. Idea . . . A wet room.

Jill   . . . Yes. Lots of renovators crammed in.

Ollie   Standing in a pool of water.

Jill and **Ollie**   Bzzzz!

Jill   It'll be exhausting. Moving so many to the right place all the time.

Ollie   We'll manage. Don't worry.

Jill   Of *course* we'll manage. But . . .

Ollie   What?

Jill   What if . . . we might want a *third* house.

Ollie   I think that's more than likely.

Jill   It's a definite. And another house after that probably.

Ollie   A place in the country.

Jill   Oh, we've *got* to have that.

Ollie   It goes without saying, sweetheart.

Jill   But . . . this house here – it took *hundreds* of renovators. Five or six houses down the line –

Ollie   It'll take thousands. I know.

Jill   Ollie . . . You and me – we'll *never* manage that.

Ollie   We will, sweetheart. Because by then . . . we'll have two sons to helps us.

Jill   Of *course*! Miss Dee!

Ollie and **Jill**   We'll sign!

Miss Dee   Oh, children!

Jill and **Ollie** *sign contract.*

Miss Dee   Now, all the furniture stays here. It will be sold and the proceeds – along with the money from the sale of the house – will be put directly into your bank account. You start your new house exactly as you started this one. From scratch.

Jill   That's what we want.

Ollie   I'll just get Benjy –

Miss Dee   He's already in the car. Fast asleep, the little lamb. Now rush along, children. You've got a long drive ahead of you.

Ollie *and* **Jill** *embrace her.*

They leave.

Slight pause.

Slowly **Miss Dee** *turns and studies everyone.*

Miss Dee   Did you hear them earlier? 'Oh, we imagined people to talk to and there you all were!' Ha! As if *they* had anything to do with it! What do you think brought you all here? Eh? Seeing a flyer for a play? A friend saying, 'Oh, we really must "check this out"!' Oh, no. You're here because *I* summoned you. Why? Because I have a bagful of new contracts . . .

Takes contracts from bag.

Children! Allow me to introduce myself. My name is Miss Dee and I would like – with your permission, of course – to talk about a subject that is very close to my heart. Namely . . . dream homes!

Blackout.

 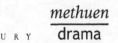 

For a complete catalogue
of Bloomsbury Methuen Drama
titles write to:

Bloomsbury Methuen Drama
Bloomsbury Publishing Plc
50 Bedford Square
London WC1B 3DP

or you can visit our website at:
www.bloomsbury.com/drama